The Rough Beast: Psych Everyday Life

The past continues to operate powerfully, wordlessly, in that less conscious part of our human mind and can trip us up unexpectedly. We can perceive and respond to situations in ways which are more to do with early experiences than the present. We can push from mind what we would rather not know. Feelings such as doubt and sadness can seem too weak; envy and anger, too bad; feeling small and in any way in need, could leave us too vulnerable.

Though most will never have their own experience of psychoanalysis (or less intensive psychoanalytic psychotherapy), psychoanalytic ideas can be profoundly helpful in making sense of ourselves. Having some access to those more hidden parts of our human mind, we can feel more alive, more real and less likely to act out in unexpected ways.

An accessible, sympathetic and challenging guide, *The Rough Beast: Psychoanalysis in Everyday Life* is for all those who are curious and sceptical as to what, why and how psychoanalytic understanding is useful in everyday life.

Denise Cullington is a psychoanalyst in private practice in Oxford, UK. She trained at the Institute of Psychoanalysis, the Tavistock Clinic, London and as a clinical psychologist. Prior to that she lived and painted in the US and in Puerto Rico.

Her book *Breaking Up Blues* (2008, Routledge) brought analytic thinking to the task of managing break-up and divorce. It was described by Steve Biddulph, author of *Raising Boys and Manhood*, as: "full of that kind of concrete but gradual, hard-earned human growth. The basic premise – that there are no easy routes or short-cuts – is so heartening to read in a world where that's all people look for. You really faced the human condition, and in doing so empowered your readers."

In memory of Anne Cullington Jones (1949–2013).
Sister, rival, beloved.

The Rough Beast: Psychoanalysis in Everyday Life

Denise Cullington

Routledge
Taylor & Francis Group

LONDON AND NEW YORK

First published 2019
by Routledge
2 Park Square, Milton Park, Abingdon, Oxon OX14 4RN

and by Routledge
52 Vanderbilt Avenue, New York, NY 10017

Routledge is an imprint of the Taylor & Francis Group, an informa business

© 2019 Denise Cullington

British Library Cataloguing in Publication Data
A catalogue record for this book is available from the British
Library

Library of Congress Cataloging in Publication Data
Names: Cullington, Denise, 1952- author.
Title: The rough beast: psychoanalysis in everyday life/Denise
Cullington.
Description: Abingdon, Oxon; New York, NY: Routledge, 2018. |
Includes bibliographical references and index.
Identifiers: LCCN 2018018197 (print) | LCCN 2018029308
(ebook) | ISBN 9780429450235 (Master eBook) | ISBN
9781138614956 | ISBN 9781138614956(hardback) | ISBN
9781782203674(pbk.) | ISBN 9780429450235(ebk)
Subjects: LCSH: Psychoanalysis.
Classification: LCC BF175 (ebook) | LCC BF175 .C855 2018
(print) | DDC 150.19/5–dc23
LC record available at https://lccn.loc.gov/2018018197

ISBN: 978-1-138-61495-6 (hbk)
ISBN: 978-1-782-20367-4 (pbk)
ISBN: 978-0-429-45023-5 (ebk)

Typeset in Times New Roman
by Integra Software Services Pvt. Ltd.

You have not grown old, and it is not too late
to dive into your increasing depths
where life calmly gives out its own secret.
                    Rainer Maria Rilke

Contents

Permissions

Acknowledgements

This book is a result of my debt to psychoanalysis.

I was helped as a patient in analysis over two periods of time. I had the great fortune of training and learning in the Adult Department of the Tavistock Clinic, and subsequently at the Institute of Psychoanalysis (London).

In the years afterwards, I learned from my patients in NHS settings, privately, and in continuing discussions with colleagues. My thanks in particular go to Martha Papadakis, Martin Miller, John Steiner, Edna O'Shaughnessy, Betty Joseph, Elizabeth Spillius, Kate Barrows and Pip Garvey.

There were many who supported me through the long process of writing until the story slowly revealed itself. Several non-analytic friends read the book and gave thoughtful feedback: Jennie Karle, Mary Ayres, Jane Bingham, Robert Bullard, Ruth Burch, Paul Goodman, Katie Roberts, Miriam Scott Pete Wallis and Rose-Anne Varley. Analytic colleagues who read parts of the book include Susannah Taffler, Erika Bard, Jim Rose, Elizabeth Spillius, Sally Weintrobe, Jenny David, Marianne Parsons, Lydia Tischler, Domenico Di Ceglie, and Judith Jackson. Nevertheless, the responsibility for the presentation of ideas remains mine. Ismail Abushamma was an enthusiast and indexer. Rod Tweedy and Oliver Turnbull at Karnac were helpful and efficient, as were later, Elliott Morsa, Adam Guppy, Yvonne Doney and Ana Maldonado at Routledge. My parents gifted me a capacity for perseverance. My family bore with me generously. To these, and more, I offer my thanks.

Finally, I would like to thank my patients, with whom I shared the struggle to wait, notice, and understand more. I am grateful to those who allowed me to include a part of their story: it is not easy being approached in this way and many of those who were agreed – and some, who did not.

Denise E. Cullington

... in a world he changed
simply by looking back with no false regrets;
all he did was to remember
like the old and be honest like children.

He wasn't clever at all: he merely told
the unhappy Present to recite the Past
like a poetry lesson till sooner
or later it faltered at the line where

long ago the accusations had begun,
and suddenly knew by whom it had been judged,
how rich life had been and how silly,
and was life-forgiven and more humble ...

and showed us what evil is, not, as we thought,
deeds that must be punished, but our lack of faith,
our dishonest mood of denial,
the concupiscence of the oppressor ...

... (he) would give back to
the son the mother's richness of feeling:
but he would have us remember most of all
to be enthusiastic over the night,
not only for the sense of wonder
it alone has to offer, but also
because it needs our love.
      W. H. Auden, 'In Memory of Sigmund Freud'

Prologue

What rough beast, its hour come round at last,
Slouches towards Bethlehem to be born?[1]
W. B. Yeats, ('The Second Coming' 1919)

This is the book I would have liked to have read when I was 18 and full of anxieties that seemed so alarming it was almost certainly better to push them out of mind. It would have been so helpful back then (or at any later stage) to discover that discomfort, what is *rough*, might be tolerated, known about, and learned from.

So here is that book: a guide to what, why, and how psychoanalytic ideas are useful in everyday life. I hope to make a complicated subject simple – without over-simplifying it. It is not a textbook, or a substitute for an experience of being in psychotherapy or an analysis – but it offers tools that may be valuable in thinking about and understanding yourself better.

Some will want to know more about how Freud and other analysts reached their conclusions: *Does it make sense? What's the evidence? Isn't it rubbish?* Others will prefer to jump to the key psychoanalytic ideas and what they may offer.

I have tried to find a way between these two. It is not essential to read straight through in the order that I have chosen. It is possible to skip or skim and, maybe, come back later to check up on earlier parts.

Note

1 Yeats wrote this poem in the aftermath of the First World War and the Easter Uprising in Ireland and the violence, terror, and death that had been unleashed, but also in reaction to the loss of Maude Gonne, the woman he loved, to a Republican hero. Even in times of relative peace, there is still that wilder, fearful, *rougher* aspect of us all, just out of conscious sight – and which can trip us up unexpectedly.

Chapter 1

Introduction

What is psychoanalysis?

As children we learn what is wanted and admired and what most certainly is not – and that, we cover over. We cover it from ourselves as much as from anyone else, being busy, positive, and not thinking: just getting on with things. Only at odd moments of external stress, exhaustion, in dreams, in the middle of a row, or having taken too much alcohol or other drugs does something *rougher* slip out.

Previous generations kept a 'stiff upper lip' in times when warfare and early deaths provided much to cause a lip to wobble. For a later generation the injunction was to be 'laid back' and 'cool'.

And now? Presentation rules. Positive thinking: keep the outside glossy and hope the inside will shift to match. Magazine articles and many self-help books offer the message that a makeover – a new haircut, new clothes, new interest, a job, car, house or affair – should mean the Good Life and the end to doubt, anxiety or restless nagging resentment.

But, too often, the enthusiasm passes and you are left with that same old flawed you. The outside might indeed look better. If you have been encouraging yourself more, being more active, you could indeed have a new spring in your step – but even so, might still feel that there is a less airbrushed *you* that has not gone away. You can end up feeling inauthentic: that the inside and the out do not match. Unwanted rougher feelings still lurk: feelings of anxiety, doubt, and depression – and resentment that you should suffer these feelings when luckier others apparently do not.

At any one time, one in six of us could be diagnosed as suffering from clinical depression or anxiety; a further tenth rely on alcohol or other drugs to manage their mood (Layard, 2006). We suffer stress-related and psychosomatic ailments, and GPs can frequently find no physical cause for the many who go to them for help with aches and pains. Women and men, adolescent and adult, can exercise and diet their bodies into particular desired shapes, hoping to find relief. Many take prescription or non-prescription drugs to achieve the required liveliness or to smooth over disturbance.

The problem is that managing what is unwanted by pushing it from mind leaves you emptier and with fewer links to your emotional self. *Not knowing* might feel safer – but leaves you feeling less alive. You may hope for closeness and intimacy – but can fear letting in a partner, family or friends in case they see this *rougher* you. It is all too easy to end up under a layer of armour, defended against an inner *beast* that, unattended, remains inarticulate – slouching and suspicious. Knowing your less-than-perfect self might be a blow but, when you can spend less energy covering it over, it can also be freeing – making it possible to feel more alive, closer to yourself and to others.

This book offers psychoanalytic ideas for discovering that lesser known part of the mind. Just as Einstein's discoveries are fundamental to modern physics (even if parts have been elaborated on and others superseded), so too are Freud's ideas, some dating back well over one hundred years, and developed in revisions by Freud and by other analysts. I bring ideas of Freud, Melanie Klein, Anna Freud, Winnicott, Bion and later analysts to help us notice what goes on in us all and the impact of that as we go through life. I do not mention by name the many analysts from the British tradition whose development of these ideas permeate this account.

Neither do I speak of analysts such as Jung, or other analytic thinkers whose traditions are not mine. There may be much to say, but I am not the person to write of them and there is enough here for a rich feast.

I bring brief examples from patients, all of whose details have been changed in some way to protect their identity. I also use clinical examples from Freud, Klein, Winnicott and Anna Freud and offer more detailed accounts of some of them in the Appendices. For those interested, they can be read in the original too.

As in an analysis or psychotherapy, my aim is not so much to give a lecture on psychoanalysis but to offer an experience of being listened to, and listening to yourself, in a psychoanalytic way. It entails circling round ideas, coming across them from different angles, which may only slowly begin to make some sort of emotional sense.

So what is psychoanalysis?

We do not function only logically and rationally. There is another parallel part of mind that is more primitive, passionate and impulsive, governed by wishful thinking. Psychoanalysis offers access to that deeper layer.

It does not supplant the findings from religious faith, meditative techniques, cognitive–behaviour therapy, or neurophysiology: it enriches them, fundamentally. It describes something that is about an emotional truth rather than a logical, rational truth. So something can seem logically ridiculous and yet still strike a distant, uneasy chord.

This other part of the mind is less available to the conscious mind, in part because it stems from a pre-history before there were words in which to think and encode: a time when the baby we once were experienced bodily sensations and biologically driven impulses, and attempted to make meaning of the world – of the good and the bad, and what or who could be trusted. It is an infantile mind.

But, Freud argued, this part of mind is also less available because what is to be discovered is disturbing and shameful, and we push it from our conscious mind. He described the relation between the logical, reality-orientated part of the mind (the ego) and this other impulsive, wishful-thinking one (the id) as

> *like a man on horseback, who has to hold in check the superior strength of the horse ... often a rider, if he is not to be parted from his horse, is obliged to guide it where it wants to go*
>
> (Freud, 1923, p. 25).

To benefit from that powerful, lively, self-willed, panicked and sometimes destructive aspect of ourselves, control on its own does not work.

The point is not to get rid of everything more primitive, for it is the source of liveliness, energy, who we are. It is better, however uncomfortably, to have some awareness of what goes on in us often out of conscious sight: then we have more choice, we use less energy in shutting down. Freud's *horse* (or my *rough beast*) needs to be attended to and allowed space or it may bolt, stampede or kick out unexpectedly, or give up and live disheartened in one tight, safe corner of the field.

Psychoanalytic ideas can be jargon-filled and hard to understand. However, the problem can be less that the ideas in themselves are so complicated, but more that it involves noting things about ourselves that we would rather not. It works not through practical advice, but through finding words for what is otherwise inarticulate, offering non-moralistic scrutiny.

Psychoanalysis is creative and contradictory – not surprisingly if you think of the focus of the study: our endlessly complicated human selves. There are disagreements within groups, tensions and arguments – as you might expect (and even hope for) in any lively extended family – where ideas matter. And such challenges help us to clarify ideas and to keep learning from clinical experience.

How something is taken up may differ in a consulting room in different parts of the world, but what you would be likely to find in any of those places is a very particular, careful listening, not only to the words, but to the emotional quality of what you bring and its meaning. Its thinking valuably informs many less intensive treatments: in work with adults and children, in families and in group settings.

Psychoanalysis is not perfect. It is not quick or easy. It takes time: time to wonder and for things to drift away. It takes an alertness, an interest in your own mind and its panicky evasions, a preparedness to wonder whether, at this moment in your life, what you tell yourself is unbearable might be uncomfortable but thinkable. If so, it might be possible to manage your anxieties in a different, less constrained way.

Some of what Freud said, which was so unacceptable at the time, is now simply taken for granted. Others of his ideas are still disturbing and we can want to disparage them – maybe more so if they are uncomfortably true. It is easy to be dismissive of Freud: to take one part of his ideas gained from over 40 years' clinical experience and disagree with it, ignoring how those ideas developed and changed. And ignoring, too, what astonishing food for thought his theories offer.

Does psychoanalysis work?

Analysts have always been interested in showing the power of their understanding through careful clinical case studies in the more than one hundred years since Freud first began. Many people who have had an experience of being a patient have felt subtly but deeply helped – and some feel their life has been saved.

Psychologist Kay Jamison wrote of her manic-depressive cycles, and her finding that she needed medication to stop her suicidal impulses and stabilize her mood, which then made long-term psychotherapy possible. She wrote,

> ineffably psychotherapy heals. It makes some sense of the confusion, reins in the terrifying thoughts and feelings, returns some control and hope and possibility of learning from it all. Pills cannot, do not, ease one back into reality
>
> (Jamison, 1995, pp. 88–89).

Analysts have been slow to embrace other research, arguing that techniques such as randomized controlled trials over-simplify and are intrusive on their patients. But studies have accumulated over the past 30 years that show how helpful psychoanalytic therapies can be for patients with complex and long-term difficulties (Leichsenring, 2005; Leichsenring & Klein, 2014).

So for example:

- One recent study bringing together results from twenty-three separate outcome studies, showed consistently good results for psychoanalytically based psychotherapy (Shedler, 2010a, 2010b).[1]
- Patients with chronic, treatment-resistant depression plus additional personality difficulties showed significant and stable gains as a result of weekly psychoanalytic psychotherapy over 18 months (Taylor et al., 2012; Fonagy et al., 2015).[2]
- Twice weekly psychoanalytic psychotherapy over two years was helpful with patients with complex needs who had dropped out of other forms of treatment (Bell, 2018).
- Analytic understanding was a great help in a day hospital unit for those with borderline personality disorder (Bateman, 1995).[3]

Psychoanalysis is not about *belief* and submission, but about hypothesis building and testing. Freud (and subsequent analysts) worked carefully with patients, noting and learning from experience what helped and what did not. And what is most convincing for a patient or a reader is when an idea or an example makes sudden, disturbing, gut sense.

Notes

1 Treatment resulted in symptom improvement but in wider gains too: patients improved in their sense of self, they had better impulse control, they related better to others and they developed personality resources which helped them withstand future stresses better. These gains maintained and often increased over time.
2 The Tavistock Depression Study.
3 Ideas such as splitting and projection, and of hatred of the staff coming together like a parental couple were fundamental to the understanding of the disturbing and intense feelings and enactments within the unit.

Chapter 2

Fundamental Freud

I had an overpowering need to understand something of the riddles of the world in which we live and perhaps even contribute something ...
(Freud, 1926, p. 252).

By the end of the nineteenth century, Vienna, once the capital of the Austro-Hungarian empire, had 'a stagnating social order based on a feudal Catholic tradition' (Natter, 2001). Critics condemned a 1910 Gustav Klimt exhibition for showing 'nakedness for its own sake', 'sick art', and 'highly repellent' work, as a result of which 'the moral floodgates would open' (Natter, 2001, p. 30). What Freud began to say (and Klimt depict) was often unacceptable and shocking to a hypocritical turn-of-the-century world where the number of prostitutes in Vienna was astonishingly high (Vergo, 1975), and where, in the opposite corner, was another powerful influence, Rationalism: the argument that everything was available to the conscious, logical mind.

Sigmund Freud (1856–1939)

Freud was the first born and favourite son of a young mother, Amalia, and a much older wool-merchant father. He was treated as special, his mother's *golden Sigi*, and funds for his schooling were found even after the bankruptcy of his father's business.

When Freud was two, a younger brother died – and later, in his self-analysis, Freud recalled how he was pleased at the death. When the young Sigi complained that his sister's piano practice disturbed him, the piano was removed. The family expected great things of their son and Freud too dreamed of gaining absolute success, as had his hero, the Greek emperor, Alexander.

Freud was combative. He was a Jew in an increasingly anti-Semitic Austria: at nine he witnessed his father being humiliated by passing soldiers. Anti-Semitism increased through the late 1800s, and might have slowed Freud's medical advancement. When Germany invaded Austria in 1938, the populace surprised even the Nazis by the enthusiasm of their looting, sackings, confiscation of Jewish businesses and book-burnings (including Freud's books).

Freud spent six years in neuro-physiological research before finally finishing his medical training. His earliest theories were biological: that physical tension, especially sexual frustration and inhibitions, underlie neurosis and he believed that his own headaches were in response to his frustratingly long wait to marry.

Freud analysed his own dreams, discovering in them unacceptable and hidden wishes, which fuelled his research. He began to argue that mental distress and anxiety is the result of emotional conflict: conflict between sexual impulses and morality; between loving feelings and frustrated, hateful ones; between a drive towards life and differentiation – and towards a more deathly turning away from reality.

Freud did not easily tolerate challenge, fearing that his theories were being watered down, and dissenters were ruthlessly excluded from his group, most notably Jung. Nevertheless, he was a trenchant critic of his own work, shifting his ideas in response to his clinical experience – even when it was unpopular to do so. He took the brave step of publishing one of his treatment failures, Dora,[1] because he was fascinated to learn from and discuss what had gone wrong. The development of those later ideas can be seen in his years of writing and in the many footnotes added to earlier papers.

Freud lived for 83 years, seeing the destructive impact of the First World War in Europe (and fearing for his sons in that war), the death of his daughter Sophie, and the rise of Nazism. For the last sixteen years of his life Freud suffered with cancer of the jaw and had a painful prosthesis. Even so, he stayed extraordinarily productive and, even in his last months, was working on a controversial monograph.[2]

By those last years Freud was widely acclaimed. He was seen as a liberator from the strictures of repressive social conventions of both the Catholic Church and of Rationalist thinking. His ideas influenced modernist art and literary movements. He was put forward for the Nobel prize for literature.[3] He won the Goethe prize and was made a member of the Royal Society. When, in 1932, Einstein was asked by the League of Nations to debate whether there is any way of delivering mankind from the menace of war, his chosen discussant was Freud.

In 1938, the penultimate year of Freud's life, and following the Gestapo's questioning of Freud's daughter, Anna, the family moved to England. Leonard Woolf, meeting him in that last year described him as

> Not only a genius, but also, unlike many geniuses, an extraordinarily nice man … There was something of him as of a half-extinct volcano, something sombre, suppressed, reserved. He gave me the feeling which only a very few people whom I have met gave me, a feeling of great gentleness, but behind the gentleness, great strength
>
> (Woolf, 1961, pp. 168–169).

The unconscious

Freud did not claim to have discovered the unconscious – he thought that great playwrights, poets and novelists had done this, and that is why their work can speak so powerfully to us. But it was Freud who first charted its role for good and bad in our emotional life.

There are some things that we do not recall until something sensory – a sight, smell, a snatch of music – brings a flood of memory back as, for Marcel Proust, did the taste of madeleine cakes. These past memories may have been dormant for years, but there is no active block to their conscious recall. There are other memories, wishes and ideas that stir up feelings of shame, guilt and vulnerability (particularly sexual and hostile ones), and energy is expended in keeping such ideas and impulses from the conscious mind.

In his own self-analysis, Freud paid careful attention to his dreams, to thoughts that came to mind and which could so easily slip away. One famous dream of his shows how wish fulfilment operates.

At a party, Irma, a young woman patient of his, complains to him of her continuing symptoms. Freud tells her that if she still suffers it is her fault because she has not accepted his solution. As Irma insists the pain is worse, he looks inside her mouth and is alarmed to see white nodules in her throat. He gets other doctors to advise him. It turns out that one way or another all the other doctors are at fault, not him. And one, Otto, has given her an injection – 'and the syringe was probably not clean' (Freud, 1900, pp. 106–121). Freud did not write all his associations to the dream, but he was clear that the dream was an attempt to exonerate himself from guilt in relation to patients.[4]

Defences can be necessary and helpful in protecting against emotional pain. It is when they are used rigidly, impermeably, that they can cause problems. Then they emerge in apparently inexplicable ways as symptoms and inhibitions.

Early on, Freud spent nine months working in Paris with renowned neuro-physiologist Charcot, who was having some success using hypnosis to treat women in-patients with hysterical symptoms (such as paralyses, nervous coughs and tension pains, without any physiological foundation). There was much for women to feel frustrated about in the patriarchal society of Freud's day. With their passions funnelled into such a narrow channel, it is no surprise that conflict and frustration in women erupted in a variety of distorted, bodily ways.

On his return from Paris, Freud heard of the work of a senior colleague, Breuer, who had helped a wealthy young woman, **Anna O**, cure herself of hysterical symptoms by 'chimney sweeping': actively recalling the moment at which the symptom had first occurred and the emotional struggle involved (Breuer & Freud, 1893).

> So the young woman pieced together how her nervous cough first occurred while nursing her sick father, hearing dance music and wishing she could dance too: a shameful wish she wanted to suppress. Bringing these associations and wishes to light relieved many of her symptoms.

The story became more complicated, Anna O becoming more demanding of her physician, refusing to eat unless fed by him and later going into a 'labour' of his wished-for baby.

Still, it seems that the work Anna O had done with Breuer had helped her, for she did well and went on to have a career in analytic social work with children[5]

Freud, meanwhile, was fascinated: he thought a patient's loving feelings towards her physician were not due to the 'charms of his own person' but rather were a defence against facing painful reality: the frustration and hatred that he, the physician, was not *hers* (Freud, 1915a).

It is not only loving and possessive feelings that are suppressed, but hostile ones, too. In the following case history, a young man faced tormenting anxieties that his hostile feelings would cause terrible damage to those he also, ambivalently, loved.

The Rat Man (Freud, 1909a)

This 27-year-old man had obsessional fears that various disasters, including a horrific rat torture, would happen to the young woman he continued to call 'his lady' (though she had twice rejected him) and to his (by then dead) father, unless he acted to prevent them. While logically the young man knew his fears were ridiculous, he felt compelled to act in 'mad' obsessional ways to forestall the dreaded outcome.

He was excited by the possibility of the disasters, which expressed his hostile id impulses towards the rejecting lady and his father (who, he believed, inhibited his sexuality) – and simultaneously he was appalled by it.

Hateful, murderous wishes and his horror of them meant that the young man was consumed with anxious, displaced guilt, describing himself as like a rat: *such a nasty, dirty little wretch apt to bite.*

The Rat Man's love for 'his lady' was narcissistic: it was for someone who *should* be 'his', since he wished it, rather than bear the painful reality that, after two rejections, she really was not. Instead he stayed stuck, refusing to accept reality: she remained *his*: both loved and desired – and hated and punished.

It is easy to feel critical of the Rat Man and agree that he is indeed a wretch. The painful thing to notice is that we too share similar ruthless feelings, where we want the world and others to revolve around us and feel aggrieved, attacking and then anxiously guilty, when they do not.

Controversial Freud

Some of Freud's thinking has been challenged. It is easy to assume that if one part of Freud's understanding looks dubious, then his whole theory is undermined.

Surely it's not relevant now?

In many external ways, life is different now. Women and men are less straitjacketed into strictly 'feminine' and 'masculine' roles. Parenting can be shared in male and female couples, as well as in heterosexual ones. There are more single-parent families.

Still, emotionally there are the same frustrations to manage: the same conflicts between loving feelings and hating ones; of wanting to have it all and the reality of separateness and exclusion; between wishful thinking and the demands of sharing and caring for others. We still use familiar defences to protect ourselves.

Didn't Freud ignore evidence of abuse in hysteria?

Freud first thought that hysterical symptoms were a response to sexual abuse which had been repressed and that recalling such abuse to conscious mind would effect a cure. He put considerable pressure on his patients to remember such events. Freud first used hypnosis, then physical pressure on the patient's head. Finally, he asked patients to report what came to mind – to free associate.

Over time, Freud's view modified. He thought that while abuse *had* happened in some cases, what caused hysterical symptoms was a conflict between a wish, often a sexual one, which was unacceptable to the conscious mind and was, therefore, pushed out of mind – such as in Anna O's wish to dance (1905, p. 18).

Some have criticized Freud's change of view, arguing that he ignored real abuse, possibly for economic reasons, to avoid alienating the fathers or husbands of such patients (Masson, 1992; Crews & Crews, 1995). An opposing argument has also been made: that Freud put too much pressure on his patients to 'remember' abuse and that he was more likely to have found more false positives than ignored real abuse (Webster, 2005).

What about the Oedipus complex and women?

Most analysts would argue that the Oedipus complex is still powerfully relevant now. While Freud's views on women have been fundamentally challenged, I argue why they can still be food for thought in Chapters 11 and 12.

What about when an interpretation is unconvincing?

In his case studies, Freud can be so busy telling a fascinating clinical story that he can leave a reader not sure how he got there because he has made too many connections of which we, the reader, know only a small part. One example is in Freud's interpretation of a famous dream.

The Wolf Man (Freud, 1918)[6]

An immensely wealthy and emotionally deprived 23-year-old Russian, Sergei Panchikoff, came to Freud suffering from symptoms of depression, suspicion and feeling not *quite alive*. Physically, he needed daily enemas to manage constipation.

> The year prior to coming to Freud, the young man's elder sister had killed herself, followed some months later by his father. Consciously, he experienced no feelings of loss, but instead was pleased that he did not have to share the family wealth with his sister.
>
> At 4 years old, following a dream, the little boy had developed a phobia of wolves and would scream at a picture of a wolf standing on its hind legs (which his sister delighted in showing him) and he feared *being eaten* by one.

Freud treated the Wolf Man for over four years, describing him as 'unassailably entrenched behind an attitude of obliging apathy' (p. 11). Freud set a termination date four months in the future. In that time they worked to unpick his childhood dream that had sparked off his wolf phobia.

His 4-year-old dream was of *the windows opening and he saw six or seven white wolves with big tails, sitting in a tree, very still, and looking intently. He feared being eaten by them.*

> The young man's association was to a childhood story of wolves, where an old (father) wolf is tricked and left tail-less. But there is a threat of punishment: the wolves might eat him.

With his patient, Freud reconstructed events in the following way: that the childhood dream harked back to an experience when the boy had been 18 months old, sick and therefore sleeping in his parent's bedroom.

> He had seen (*the windows opening*) his parents active in intercourse (the opposite of *very still*), his father entering his mother from behind, and in this way had found evidence of genital difference: if not everyone has a penis, might his be attacked as a result of his hostile wishes towards his wolf/father?

This reconstruction of the boy's discovery of sexual difference can seem dramatic, but not necessarily convincing. Freud thought that his patient was as likely to have gained evidence from watching sheep rutting on the family estate, but his patient had 'contempt' for any other possibility.[7]

Still, the interpretative work done as a result of this dream (the child's angry, attacking feelings towards his depressed, tail-less father and his fears of punishment) helped the young man finish his studies. He returned to Russia where he set up a law practice and married.

Corroboration

Recent neurological studies confirm Freud's clinically based discoveries of the disconnection between the organising and verbal capacities (associated with the frontal regions) and the more instinctive, emotional functions (associated with the limbic system and deeper areas of the brain).

- This is so with studies of decision-making (Kahneman, 2003),[8] memory (Kandel, 1999, 2006),[9] and attention (Shevrin et al., 2013).[10]
- Analytic studies of the impact on patients with brain injuries found a pattern consistent with the unconscious and repression (Kaplan-Solms & Solms, 2000).[11]
- Those with high background anxiety are disproportionately affected by unconsciously perceived threats (Etkin et al., 2004).

Freud was picking up clinically what was later discovered neurologically.

The point is not that he got everything *right*, but that he was astonishing in what he did get hold of. Freud offered a rich basis on which to continue to work clinically, to keep developing ideas in response to the evidence and to an ongoing debate, which continues still.

Notes

1 See page 24.
2 Moses and Monotheism (1939).
3 By a prestigious group including Thomas Mann, Bertrand Russell, Julian Huxley, Lytton Strachey and A. S. Neill.
4 What Freud left unsaid was that Irma also represented Emma Eckstein, a patient his then-friend and confidant Fliess had operated on, leaving gauze in her nose with near-fatal effect, and in the dream, Freud exonerates him. The injection is also likely to refer to Freud's talented friend and colleague, Fleischl-Marxov, whom Freud had advised to use cocaine to help him withdraw from a morphine addiction for chronic pain. His friend had injected cocaine, became very addicted to it and had died some years earlier at only 45. Freud was plagued with guilt. The doctor represented by Otto had criticized him for his early endorsement of cocaine. Now Otto becomes the one who is at fault.
5 A longer account of Anna O is in Appendix A.
6 See Appendix E.
7 He later rebutted this idea.
8 There is one slow, logical system (associated with the frontal lobes), another which is fast and impulsive (associated with the limbic system and the more primitive brain stem).
9 One system is verbal, rational and explicit (associated with the frontal lobes). Attention is needed to encode this memory and, when under stress, this verbal memory is impeded.
   Another is primary process, impulsive and emotional (associated with the brain stem). It includes alertness to danger and a freeze reaction. Recall is not in words but via associations and in gut feeling. This second system has a rapid, direct connection to the cortex, bypassing verbal encoding.

10 Studies suggest one system for conscious attention; the other for unconscious vigilance.

Presentation of conflict words and images affect a different part of the brain when presented too fast for conscious recognition than when presented for longer, consistent with the workings of repression. (These findings were sufficient to convince philosopher of science and critic of psychoanalysis, Grunbaum, that repression had been proved (Barry & Fisher, 2014).)

11 So a patient with right temporo-parietal damage did not acknowledge that his left arm was paralysed, typical of damage to that area. It could be seen as just organic, but when his analyst interpreted to him the pain of noticing that his arm was paralysed and that he feared whether it would recover or not, he responded with despair: '*Look* at my arm – what am I going to *do* if it doesn't recover?' He was silent for a long while: then he reverted to his former apparently indifferent state.

Chapter 3

How does psychoanalysis work?

> The discovery that you have a MIND is always a shock: you never know
> what the strange object is going to turn out to be.
>
> (Bion, 1991, p. 226)

At a deep level, mostly out of conscious mind, the past continues to haunt us –
and the more so, the more it is pushed from the mind. We *repeat* (in our
actions) rather than *remember* (Freud, 1914a, p. 130).

Psychoanalysis has built up a model of early experience from the first days
onwards: some from infant observation and work with young children, but in
particular from clinical work with that more disturbed part of adult patients –
and of us all.

That model of the baby and young child brought by Freud, developed by later
analysts and corroborated by later research, is of a baby with his own particular
sensitivities, inevitable conflicts and frustration to be faced, and defences against
knowing of these unacceptable wishes. There is also a mother, with her internal
resources, external support – and the impact of this on her baby.

Some feelings and experiences come from early on: from a time before there
were words in which to think or remember. These impressions may be experienced more as a gut feeling, an expectation or a mood, and are expressed in the
body and in action. We experience those same unruly thoughts, feelings and
wishes – conscious and unconscious – but we cover them over and rationalize
them. Sometimes they burst out unexpectedly. Sometimes they quietly go on
influencing our attitudes out of conscious awareness.

Psychoanalytic thinking means keeping hold of ideas, even when they are
disturbing, rather than smoothing them over and easing them out of conscious
mind. It means allowing thoughts in enough to feel an emotional impact rather
than keeping them at a distance, where they are not really allowed to matter.

It unscrambles and acknowledges what were real difficulties in the past and
their impact. It also means teasing apart the way we have managed such
difficulties; what we have brought – and maybe still do in the present – in ways
which keep us stuck, unable to be fully responsive to others or to ourselves.

In the end, it is not to get rid of what is not wanted but to be able to tolerate knowing what is there, to have words in which to think.

How do we access what is unconscious?

Sometimes paying particularly focused attention can reveal quite a bit about that less conscious part of the mind.

In the 1920s, feeling dissatisfied and not as engaged in life as she wanted to be, a young woman began a journal, tracking her moments of happiness and paying close attention to what she found slipping away, out of the corner of her mind (Milner, 1986). What she discovered was that her less conscious mind was

> ... not a dark and gloomy place into which only the psychoanalytic high priests had passports, but as a kind of mental activity which was different from rational thought but nonetheless an existent reality, observable just as children's conversation can be observed [and] liable to the same misunderstandings and distortions
>
> (p. 204).

She found how her

> chattering mind ... recognised only itself and was always trying to force the rest of the world to do the same ... It wanted me to be the best, cleverest, most beautiful creature, and made me feel that if I was not all of these things then I was the extreme opposite, the dregs of creation and utterly lost
>
> (p. 130).

She noticed how by making a fuss when it did not go all her own way she believed that someone (like her loved, now dead, father) would take care of her, and that in being too happy,

> I might give up my claim to that special attention which seemed to be the prerogative of the miserable
>
> (p. 120).

Looking back, she was pleased at her efforts:

> though some of these discoveries were not entirely pleasant ... they gave me a sense of being alive, but the feelings stirred up were not easy to bear, bringing with them echoes of terror and despair
>
> (p. 66).

The writer, Marion Milner, subsequently went on to train as an analyst.[1]

Free association

In analysis Freud asked patients to

> *say whatever goes through your mind. Act as though, for instance, you were a traveller sitting next to the window of a railway carriage and describing to someone inside the carriage the changing views which you see outside. Finally, never forget that you have promised to be absolutely honest, and never leave anything out because, for some reason or other, it is unpleasant to tell it*
>
> (Freud, 1913).

Freud did not expect that as patients, we would always abide by that rule: our defences would get in the way, making us deliberately or unconsciously turn away. But it is that sudden turning away, or the affect not matching what is spoken of, to which an analyst is alert.

Dreams

Freud described dreams as 'The royal road to the unconscious' (Freud, 1900, p. 627).

Dreams offer a visual, sensual picture – and, depending on the associations that come to mind, they can offer a way into our inner life. (As did Freud's Irma dream, on p. 8.) Because they deal with images rather than words, they can evade a censoring function.

We bring the images dreams offer and the thoughts and associations, which may be specific ones or more tangential: a sequence of ideas as they come to mind. Understanding what a dream might illuminate is based on the associations of the patient and of the analyst; on what has slowly emerged in the analysis and what feels authentic, or not.

Dreams can present an internal situation in a vivid way. At the end of her third year in analysis, **Jan** brought a dream:[2]

> *'I was in a big building like a railway station. Something horrible had happened, like a murder. I was on a scooter – no, I was watching a man on a scooter, someone I knew at university. His name was Juncker. He was getting away on the scooter aiming for a quiet exit. But the floor was very polished and he did not have much traction so he got off and pushed the scooter, then he went out the door.'*

Juncker, it turned out, was not a friend but someone Jan disapproved of: he was 'arrogant, hard-faced'. Her associations were to the film, *The Italian Job*: it seemed that she was not on the side of the criminal as in this film, but thought he should be caught. Jan also had an association to the German reparations post the First World War, which were severe and led to hatred and further war.

Jan was disturbed when the analyst commented that, as she had told her dream, Jan seemed confused with the hard-faced Juncker. *'I was on a scooter – no, I was watching a man on a scooter . . .'*

The following day Jan felt troubled. She did not see herself as hard-faced at all. Quite the reverse – and she detailed all the ways she was not. She thought the analyst was probably not really saying that she was completely hard-faced and bad, but that was how it felt to her. (A bit like the punitive First World War reparations.) It was difficult for Jan to shift from this position.

The analyst then spoke of Jan's dream, where the shiny floor made it hard to find traction and how that seemed to be what was happening now. It was as if a part of her, as in *The Italian Job*, did want to slip out the back door – even if there was also this other her, observing and feeling that this Juncker should be caught.

In a warmer voice, Jan commented how *her mother could get very huffy when she was criticized, and she could see how she was a bit like this too.*

However, a moment later she said she *hoped she was not like this. She thinks she is not.*

The analyst commented on this shift away. Jan laughed, but she was surprised and uneasy.

And so the work continued.

Jan's dream conveyed two very separate aspects of herself: one a rather moral, judgemental one, looking on, the other greedy, lively, demanding – and slippery.

You could say that Jan is *robbing* in her accusation that her analyst is meanly critical of her, if it leaves the *bank/analyst* with fewer assets able to help Jan understand herself. If Jan can hold on to a *Juncker*/her, who is rivalrous with her analyst and wanting to be the one with *all the goods* and the understanding, this would be painful to her – but it might not be a capital offence.

The transference

The central focus of psychoanalysis (and of less intensive psychoanalytic psychotherapy) is our internal world: not only understanding the past, but what is alive in the present.

As a patient in an analysis, we bring our conscious thoughts and ideas, the sense we have made of why we feel the disturbance we do, and our efforts to change this or to push it out of sight. We bring our account of the past: memories of early experiences and the family we grew up in; who and what was helpful or was unavailable, disturbing or frightening.

We bring what is going on in the present: our sense of ourselves, our relationships with others – partners, family, friends and those at work.

We also bring what is less conscious. We bring our habitual ways of dealing with feelings that are disturbing. What we see and experience is affected by our state of mind from moment to moment. We bring expectations and assumptions of others and of the analyst and treat him (or her) as if he *is* that particular, familiar way. Such unnoticed assumptions can have a powerful nudging impact.

What is a part of our inner world, built up from past, is transferred and is alive in the consulting room (as it also is in other relationships). This is an invaluable source of evidence in the here and now.

An analyst looks for what seems emotionally alive and true, if painful, and also what seems more of a cover-up. She (or he) brings curiosity, an interest in what links there might be between what is, or is not, said. Her purpose is not so much to reassure or to offer the 'right answer' to a dutifully receptive patient, but to help a patient be curious about their own mind and feelings, to wonder what it is that might feel so threatening, to speak to that – and also to be able to wait.

As patients, we may dutifully agree with what the analyst offers and squash down any other feelings about this. We may blank out what has been said and is unwelcome. We can quickly go on the attack and feel wounded, as Jan did above, to keep away any possibility that what the analyst says might be disturbingly true. The analyst can be felt as judgemental, mocking or simply disinterested.

And this might be accurate or it might be more to do with how we assume things to be (our internal reality). Part of the work can be in finding out how much this internal reality is really so: what is accurate and what is a distortion, chronic and limiting.

Addressing this transference relationship between patient and analyst can feel particularly alive and threatening. A classic paper likened the danger to the analyst of attacking an enemy gun emplacement, which conveys something of the passionate hostility that we can bring to bear in the service of self-protection (Strachey, 1934).

What is the difference between psychoanalysis and psychotherapy?

Psychoanalysis (and psychotherapy which is analytic) takes place at a particular place and time, a stable, safe space in which the impact of disruptions and changes can be noticed.[3]

Generally, a patient in analysis uses the couch. Just as speaking can be easier when walking or driving together, side by side, allowing silences and making it easier to speak to what is emotionally painful, so lying on the couch allows patient and analyst to have private space for thinking and dreaming: together and yet separate.

Psychoanalysis is more frequent – three, four or more sessions in a week. This makes possible a slowly evolving conversation, with time to keep things in mind and to let them slip away; to dream, to find what comes to mind and see where it leads. When sessions are more frequent it makes it more possible to stay with what is disturbing, in the face of our self-protective impulses to shut down.

In a less intensive psychotherapy, the analyst might intervene more; in the interval between sessions the patient is left more on his own, managing what is stirred up. He might be on the couch, or not. Some find that beginning with fewer sessions a week and getting an experience of the analyst can make it possible to wish for more.

Practically, there is also the question of the cost of more intensive psychotherapy or psychoanalysis. In these days, when intensive analytic therapy on the NHS is increasingly rare, and costs of living are high, then analysis can feel as if it is an impossible luxury. Even so, some feel that this help in freeing their emotional life is worth considerable sacrifice.[4]

What is a typical analytic session like?

I cannot tell you because, as a session goes along, neither patient nor analyst knows quite how it will develop. So, for example:

> A patient comes in on time – or late; he looks at the analyst in a particular way – or he looks away; he lies on the couch more or less rigidly; he breathes barely or heavily; a silence could feel reflective, anxious or defiant ... And if he remains silent, the analyst has to decide whether to wait or to intervene – and, if so, with what. (One analyst may intervene earlier; another, not. Or the same analyst may do so with a different patient, or at a different moment in the analysis.)
>
> Or the patient brings something straight away, telling of particular events or a dream – which he might seem interested in, or it might seem more like a fobbing off: he is not so interested – but maybe the analyst will be so on his behalf.
>
> The analyst notices his own feelings stirred up by what the patient brings. He (or she) might try to bring these facts and feelings together in a particular way – and the patient could react to it by letting these comments slip dully away, by being irritated and disagreeing, by agreeing dutifully but without conviction, or sometimes by bringing other thoughts.
>
> The analyst notes the impact of his intervention – and again decides whether, or what, to say. And this is the first ten minutes.

Gaining access to those less logical, less conscious parts of mind is a bit like those visual puzzles where, only if you squint or look out of the corner of your eye do you suddenly get it – and see what had been obscure. And then, all too quickly, it falls out of focus again, but at least now you know the trick of finding it when you want to. It is often invisible, but it is not a hallucination – and you can only see it in a particular mind-set.

A similar relaxed, quizzical attitude to this book could also help.

Notes

1 Marion Milner wrote under the name Joanna Field.
2 I am grateful to 'Jan' and to other patients for their permission to use some of their material to illustrate an analytic point. I have tried to mask their identity to protect their confidentiality.
3 A psychotherapy that is not analytic does not address the transference.
4 Subsidized low-cost analysis and psychotherapy is sometimes available through training organisations. The British Psychoanalytic Council lists them online. See: www.bpc.org.uk/.

Chapter 4

The downside of change

How many psychoanalysts does it take to change a light bulb?
Only one but it depends whether the light bulb really wants to change.

Really wanting to change is a mixed blessing.

It is one thing to want to be changed for the better, passively like the light bulb, quite another to risk emotional disturbance when you do not know what you will discover. It may be a relief to be helped, but if that involves noticing disturbing thoughts, feelings and wishes (conscious and unconscious) it is alarming.

It is easy then, unconsciously, and also sometimes deliberately, to turn your head away and slip back to old, familiar protective mechanisms. Sometimes it might be possible to notice how this happens; at other times it is as if this mood or thought has just flitted away. Someone else might notice an odd shift, but not you, since it has just disappeared from conscious sight.

The psychoanalyst in the light bulb joke above might be an external one, or could be an analyst *internally*: a state of some curiosity about yourself. Either way, the point of the joke is that a particular state of mind is necessary: a capacity to be somewhat open, not too defensive, and prepared (at least some of the time) to tolerate the disturbance inevitable in noticing that none of us is *only* good and in the right, or always *only* a victim.

We need that analyst (internal and external) to notice what was difficult from our past, what was stressful and what has had its impact: the sad ways in which we lost out. But if an analyst only does that, then we miss out on what we also need to know: for being calmed and reassured in itself does not help us move.

For whatever the cause, whatever the past difficulties, that stuck position is still alive and active in the present in our minds and in our expectations and assumptions of others: in feelings such as suspicion and reluctance to trust; of assuming abandonment if another even momentarily turns away; of feelings being potentially so threatening that it is easier just to turn inwards and shut down, expecting and offering little, or going on the attack.

An analytic relationship has to find some fledgling wish for help in it – however much counterbalanced by suspicion, resentment and fear of hope that might end in disappointment.

Defences

Defences are established for a good reason. The hope is to stay pain-free and protected, to manage a stressful situation in the only way that seems possible – and when challenged it can feel like an attack on all that holds us together. When defences are fiercely held it can be almost impossible to be really aware of ourselves and think: it can feel just too threatening. In that case, we can become entombed under layers of protection, any liveliness all but smothered.

Some people are not deeply defended. They might not notice the depths of their feelings or prefer to avoid them, but still those feelings are reasonably accessible, as in the following case.

> **Cheryl** came for help because she felt anxious and depressed. She had recently had a late miscarriage, which she had managed by being rational and coping – as had always seemed to work so well in the past. She told herself (as many might advise her) to 'be positive, don't dwell on it, get on and do interesting things. It's not the end of the world'.
>
> When the therapist spoke to her of the loss of her *baby*, the young woman corrected her: of course it was a *foetus* that she had lost.
>
> The therapist replied that she thought for Cheryl it *had been a baby*, alive in her mind and in her plans for the future, at which point Cheryl wept and wept.
>
> She began to allow herself painful feelings of mourning: how sad it was, how unfair, and how angry she felt about it too – all perfectly normal. She felt now that she could take this experience of the depth of her grief back to her husband and family and they could grieve together.

Cheryl's grief was very painful but, once she could allow herself to know how important it was for her, she no longer needed to defend herself against it.

Often it might be no longer clear whether what once may have been a necessary protection against disturbance is still needed in the present. It is not that we should not have defences, but it is helpful to be able to notice them and make decisions about them more consciously and flexibly.

Fierce protective defences can be present in a hidden shutting down:

> Early in her analysis, **Becky** had a dream: she was *on a cloud, asleep. It was so comfortable* – and this seemed to describe well her remote, dreamy

and unbothered state in the analysis. The more her analyst reached out, the more Becky withdrew.

When Becky was little, her mother had real external pressures and was depressed and preoccupied. Becky believed that if she made a fuss, her mother either just wouldn't notice or she would explode. So Becky shut down, and when her mother and father were more settled and tried to engage with her, she stayed withdrawn.

It seemed to her analyst that Becky was fearfully protecting herself but there was something more, too: it seemed to her that Becky felt a quiet satisfaction at seeing her analyst's efforts and pushing her away. She was cutting off a lively connection with disturbance and hungers of all kinds and any connection with her analyst. Her analyst noted and commented on this turning away, one way and another.

Painfully slowly, Becky experimented with challenging and defying her analyst more openly, rather than in her hidden withdrawal. Only then, and still suspicious, was she more able to allow in what others (including her analyst) said.

Becky began to wonder whether her mother had been as unapproachable as she had allowed herself to believe and whether, in keeping her mother out, she had deprived herself of good things, as well as protecting herself from the bad, just as happened for so painfully long a time in her analysis.

It can feel so humiliating to be noticed as being in any way not perfect. It is hard to be open and vulnerable. Remaining high up and *in the right* can seem preferable. Proving that the analyst cannot help can become more satisfying than being helped, even if it is also stressful and lonely:

Sometimes **Carol** felt touched by what her analyst said. This pleasurable state seemed to last a short time before it was lost and replaced once again by suspicion and grievance.

The analyst spoke of how it seemed as if Carol had lost the connection with a helpful her of a moment earlier, and now only had a very misunderstanding one. Carol replied furiously, *'You're saying it's all my fault!'*

There was something familiar and relentless in this pushing away. It seemed as if Carol felt not only a relief, but also a satisfaction in doing so. The analyst commenting on this felt even more inflammatory: she was now cruel and untrustworthy.

The analyst felt herself to be more guarded; less likely to put a tentative idea into words, because she anticipated that it would be batted away as either predictable, or wrong.

She was more likely to wait until she was clearer in her own mind – but then Carol would feel her analyst was making a case against her and she would become embattled.

The analyst could feel as if she was in the grip of a tyrannical patient, who condemned her if she failed in any way, and was dropped from mind when her patient had felt her to be emotionally in touch.

Just as a mother with a fractious baby turns to her partner, parents, friends, child-rearing experts and her own quiet thoughts, so the analyst had to rely on her resources, external as well as internal.

She felt less alone, more sympathetic to her patient (so bullied by a part of herself) and the anxieties that lay behind the behaviour. It also helped her feel firmer and not just retreat in the face of her patient's complaints.

The analyst spoke of how alarming it was to Carol when for a moment she felt close or trusting. This left her feeling so vulnerable that she quickly had to rubbish the connection.

It was not so much that the words used were so very different than ones she had used before, but the feeling behind them was. It was as if the analyst was closer to the feeling of vulnerability and how hard that is to bear. Carol felt more understood.

Freud's patient **Dora** is an example of how holding on to a sense of outrage and virtue got in the way of facing humiliating, but potentially freeing, truths (Freud, 1905).[1]

Eighteen-year-old Dora presented with a nervous cough, other fluctuating physical symptoms and a sudden and un-budging dislike of her former confidante whom she believed, correctly, was her father's mistress: the less well-off Frau K.

Four years earlier, Frau K's husband, Herr K, had kissed Dora, then 14, and she could still remember the pressure of his chest on her body. She subsequently developed a nervous cough. He sent her flowers daily for a year.

Two years later, on a family holiday, Herr K propositioned 16-year-old Dora: she slapped him. That afternoon, when she was having a nap, Herr K appeared in her bedroom. She subsequently took to locking the door – but the key was then removed. Dora decided not to remain with the Ks but to return home with her father.

Two weeks later, with no word from Herr K, Dora told her parents of his attempted seduction. When challenged, Herr K first promised to come and 'sort it all out'. But then he changed his mind and claimed that it was all a figment of Dora's imagination. He was backed up in this by his wife, who said that Dora 'always wanted to talk about sex'.

Dora was furious at this treble betrayal: by Herr K, Frau K and by her father's refusal to give up Frau K in the light of his daughter's distress.

Now this was certainly hurtful and humiliating and it is not surprising that Dora was furious. Freud was not surprised either.

But his key point was that Dora was more actively involved in the flirtation than she wanted to admit – and that denying this led to her furious sense of herself as a passive victim of men's voracious sexuality. He thought that Dora's memory of K's *chest* pressing against her as he kissed her when she was 14 was a displacement of her awareness of his erection. He thought that K's proposition to her was exciting as well as disturbing to the 16-year-old, who two years earlier had accepted his daily flowers and had been keen to read Frau K's illuminating sexual books.

Freud thought that if only Dora could acknowledge her apparent, but shameful, conflicting sexual feelings then she might be able to take decisions based on what she felt, rather than denying them.

Dora reported a repetitive dream that had first occurred when she was 14, following Herr K's kiss:

> *A house was on fire. My father was standing beside my bed and woke me up. I dressed quickly. Mother wanted to stop and save her jewel-case; but Father said: "I refuse to let myself and my two children be burnt for the sake of your jewel-case"*

> (Freud, 1905, p. 64).

Freud linked Dora's memory of her father coming to wake her in the night to prevent bed-wetting, with childhood masturbation linked with ideas of her father: Dora said she 'could not remember' this.

However, a few days later she

> *wore at her waist—a thing she never did on any other occasion before or after—a small reticule [a drawstring handbag] ... and, as she lay on the sofa and talked, she kept playing with it– opening it, putting a finger into it, shutting it again, and so on*

> (p. 76)

Freud told Dora that she was inadvertently confirming his suspicion of her childhood masturbation.

Two weeks later Dora walked out of treatment.

Most analysts nowadays would feel that, in his excitement about proving his theories, Freud was forcing himself on Dora, rather as Herr K had done. Looking back, Freud thought so too, and he became less directly challenging as a result.

We may wonder about the role of Dora's father in encouraging this friendship (as did Freud) and of her mother in ignoring the meaning of a daily gift of flowers. But Dora, too, had her part: she wanted to keep seeing herself as only innocent, a victim – but in a way which kept her stuck. Instead her frustration, fury and confusion were expressed through bodily symptoms such as her nervous cough. As in her dream, Dora had succeeded in protecting her *jewellery box* – her physical chastity – and her sense of aggrieved innocence, but arguably this was at the cost of the house burning down: she no longer had access to her active wishes and interests.

Some 23 years after the end of this interrupted treatment, Dora, then forty-one, consulted the analyst Felix Deutsch in New York. She had married unhappily and had one son. She remained symptomatic: frigid, complaining, bedbound, dizzy and was distraught at her now-adult son's leaving her for other sexual partners (Deutsch, 1957).

An analyst's job is to try to wonder when an interpretation is wrong, and when it is uncomfortably right, and to find a way of communicating that to a patient in a way which is tolerable – and that is not always easy. But if a way to do so cannot be found, time can pass interminably, comfortably but unproductively.

An analytic attitude

Being so frantically condemning of failure and weakness can make it dangerous to notice any rougher feelings in ourselves. It is helpful to be able to find a less severe stance.

The poet U. A. Fanthorpe described her particular warm yet tough approach to her poems – those products of her unconscious, her crafted thoughts and feelings. She said of her poems,

> As usual when they're together and bound, I feel ashamed of them . . . like a mother with a whole clutch of unsatisfactory children. I've tried to speak of them with *a father's fondness, a mother's stern regard for the truth*. But in the end they walk into the world on their own feet . . .
>
> (Fanthorpe, 1992, my emphasis)

We, too, do better with a combination of a stern regard for truth and fondness – whether we have been lucky enough to find them from real parents, or not. Fondness is a great help and reassurance. When we learn anything (learning to walk, ride a bike, play an instrument), sympathy, empathy helps when we fall or fail. We have not been stupid to try. We need to know the risks and take as much care as possible, within the limits of our skill.

But fondness on its own doesn't help us engage with the world as it is, in all its bruising reality. We need to hear another truth too, an emotional truth: that falling or failing is painful but not necessarily intolerable. Sometimes the hurt is more to do with shock or humiliation, rather than the actual bruises received. And in a universe where we are not the centre, the one and only, many face much worse: bruises, doubt and loss are a part of the scenery. With fondness as well as a firm regard for truth it becomes easier to kick ideas around to see what disturbing sense they might make, rather than just kicking them out.

In an analysis, it is of great help if we can hold on to some fond but firm stance which makes it more possible to withstand the pull to remaining cocooned, untroubled and right.

The point in an analysis (and in this book) is not to be credulous or a true believer. It is not about handing yourself over to be 'done to' or to be 'done-over'. And if you do, you would probably find an analyst who wondered what you were up to, having to be (at least on the surface) so terribly good and compliant. On the other hand, you can keep yourself so safely sceptical that you miss out on what may be disturbing – but enlivening, too.

In the long term, only if you can cautiously hold on to what makes some fleeting disturbing sense is it possible to be open to a new opportunity. Things can be born in mind that might feel very painful but are possibly not a disaster. You begin to feel something inside which is firmer – a capacity to know your thoughts and feelings more, without them being in pieces and leaving you confused or dreading attack.

At this moment, when some of the fierce protective chaff settles, the quality of the analytic encounter shifts. As in *Portnoy's Complaint* where the writer engages his analyst (and his reader) with a long, entertaining saga of his parents, his community, his sexuality, his masturbation with a piece of liver ... and finally, in the last lines of the book, his analyst is heard saying in a heavy European accent, *and now shall we begin*? (Roth, 1969).

Note

1 And see Appendix B.

Part I

Analytic understanding of early life

The child is father of the man

(Freud, 1940, p. 63).

As in archaeology – where layers of civilizations are discovered, built upon the ruins of earlier ones – so Freud described how under the more visible surface layers of our human rational civilization are our earliest, wordless, infantile and later child stages of development. These inform our assumptions and behaviour, often out of conscious awareness.

To make some sense of those more inaccessible parts of our human mind, we need to begin with an account of that baby we once were: what went on before there were words in which to remember or think, but which can affect us in powerful and subtle ways? It is a story of passionate sensations and impulses that come from within, of pressures and conflicts inevitable in development, and of emotional help received which affects how we perceive our world and the resources we have.

This way of understanding early development, gained through clinical experience, is also supported by infant observation, and later neonatal and child development studies.

Chapter 5

The baby

A child sees the face of its mother, and it sees it in a completely different way as other people see it … sees it from very near … for a little while only sees a part of the face of its mother, it knows only one feature and not another, one side and not the other [and in his way Picasso knows faces as a child knows them, and the head and the body]

(Stein, on Picasso, 1959).

Imagine a baby, like the one you once were.

You have been developing in one familiar space – and now, all of a sudden, you are in another altogether.

Sense impressions come from all around. There are the sounds of your mother's voice, and her heartbeat when she holds you against her, which are familiar from the womb. You are held in her arms, as once you were enveloped inside her. There are the sights as you gaze intently around, particularly at the faces who bend towards you, within your focal range: just the right one to see your mother's face as she feeds you in her lap or at her breast.

You have no model yet of what to expect, or much of a mind in which to think; no words in which to describe things to yourself. You have no sense yet of an inside or out.

Still, you register impulses and experiences in a rudimentary way: safe/ threat, good/bad. You have biological impulses to latch onto a nipple: to connect to a *something*. Even in the first hours you can recognize the smell of your mother's breast milk (MacFarlane, 1975).

There is some familiarity and comfort: you are not falling; you are safe.

But then that calm state shifts: you become uncomfortable. (It could be that you are hungry or tired; too cold or too hot; disturbed by the passing of faeces or the discomfort of a wet nappy. You may be alarmed by stimuli from outside or by your hands, which flail in ways they did not in the tight space of the womb.)

But you don't yet know the source of this discomfort.

You struggle to make it all right. You suck your fingers as you might have in the womb – and expect that this will fill your belly, as once it seemed to do. Now it no longer does, or not for long. As that discomfort grows, so does your fear.

Your body struggles: your back arches, your hands and legs kick out, your adrenalin rises, your cries become wails – and this is even more frightening.

If you had words to describe the experience to yourself (and you don't yet) they might be *Something awful is happening! You are helpless! Nothing will make it all right again!*

And then, all being well, help comes.

Someone looking on would see that you are picked up, held and soothed. Your nappy is changed, you are fed or held and rocked – and, as your sobs subside and your muscles ease, suddenly all is well again, for now.

From your point of view in these earliest weeks, it will not seem that help has arrived from outside, but rather that you were in one experience which was *good* and safe, and then suddenly in another terrifying, hateful, *bad* one. What is *good*, you put in your mouth and want to be yours. What is *bad*, you hope to get rid of outside of you, as you spit out unwanted food or push out faeces.

With repeated experiences of the crooning and the holding, that baby/you build up a memory of this soothing *good* experience, hold it inside and have it to help you. You are becoming more settled.

If your mother is less able to offer the empathic support you need (because her emotional resources are fewer, she has less support herself, or copes with more external pressures), you face more frustration and deprivation, more panic and rage – but you have to manage alone.

Freud describes the baby's bodily taking in of the world, drinking it in with his eyes and with his mouth (in the *oral stage*). The baby is under the sway of instinctual *id* impulses, of hungers and discomforts, of intense feelings of bliss – and of frustration and fury when is wishes do not make it so and when sucking his thumb does not fill his belly. This instinctual state is primitive, impulsive, forceful, wishful thinking. It is non-logical; not mediated by words and time has little meaning.

He wants to be the baby – and he is not, absolutely. This is a crushing narcissistic blow.

Over the first weeks and months, the baby discovers what is under his control and what, infuriatingly, is not; what are his goods and what are those of others; what is inside him and what is outside. In these discoveries, a more logical, problem-solving, reality-orientated ego develops alongside the wishful-thinking id. By the second year of life, he can move about bodily and has increasing awareness of, and control of, his full bowel and bladder: he can offer his goods – and also withhold them and excitedly, defiantly, say *no!* and *shan't!* in the *anal stage.*

These two aspects of mind, the impulsive wishful thinking one and the reality based one, are often in conflict and the rational ego has only partial control over powerful, instinctual id impulses. This is true not only for children, but for adults, too. We don' t just outgrow it. However much we ignore it, there is still something strong, wild and biologically driven underneath.

Melanie Klein (1882–1965)

Working clinically with adult patients, Freud felt there was a prehistory which he could not reach.

Analyst Melanie Klein showed a remarkable determination to get to this, which seemed so vital and yet tantalisingly inaccessible. She was able to gain access to the ideas and fears of young children by observing their play with simple, small toys, and their drawings: whether a child was inhibited and anxious in his play, or free to express aggressive, as well as loving, feelings.

Klein speaks of the infant in the first weeks and months of his life. In this time the baby is making sense of his world through his sense impressions, as in the description above of the infant (and Picasso) looking intently at one part of a mother's face – and then another aspect of her comes startlingly into focus.

She describes this as like an experience of a good breast and a separate one that is bad. She calls this inevitable but terrifying developmental state of mind 'paranoid–schizoid', which conveys both the terror and hatred of the bad experience, and its loneliness.

Separateness and conflict

Slowly, and piecemeal, you notice that wishful thinking does not fill your belly. Rather, it is your mother's presence (or other familiar carer) who smiles and calls out to you, who responds to your calls and smiles. *There's the smile, the face. Now it's gone. Where is she? Ah there, back again!*[1]

You discover that the source of help and relief is a whole figure, separate from you. It is her absence that feels so alarming, so hateful.

This is a mixed blessing.

Like any baby reaching out to something interesting and putting it in his mouth, you want to grab these good things for yourself. You may be relieved and grateful for what she offers – but at the same time you want control of it, and not her.

This is a source of painful conflict. For if your mother is a whole figure, then the one the baby and toddler/you make demands on and exhaust, the one you attack in terror and rage and out of envy, is her.

Hated as your mother is, as well as loved, you can fear the loss of her love that is so vital to you. You can fear for the damage done to the mother you also love and want to repair her – but even so, you will still struggle with the familiar hostile impulses stirred up by frustration, envy and jealousy. (Klein calls these depressive anxieties.)

> Then it can be preferable to revert to the more primitive, black and white (paranoid–schizoid) state of mind, where the goodness is all in you and the bad is felt to be outside. But as you go on the attack once again, you lose any sense of a *good mother* within to help with your fear and loneliness.

Sharing

An additional source of provocation and rage is the awareness that your mother shares her goods. She has relationships with others: with her partner, with other siblings and maybe with a new baby – and in this you are on the outside looking on.

> By the end of the first year you have more physical control: you lift your head, you crawl, stand, then walk – however much you fall. You can move towards – and run away from. You begin to have control of your bowels and your bladder: you are able to let go, and to hold inside. You can say 'no' and 'shan't'. You can grab things for yourself, particularly if anyone else shows interest in them, too.
>
> You find that there are limits. You are told 'no'. You have to wait, to share. You mustn't snatch or smack – even though you want to. You must go to bed even when the adults continue to have an interesting time downstairs (or in the bedroom).
>
> You may be delighted to build a separate relationship with your father: one which might be less tied up with infantile feeding and holding, but more with tossing in the air and revealing an exciting new life out there. But there is a problem, for he is also the one who shares and claims your mother. You may still feel yourself to be the apple of her eye – but you are not *all the time*! Then, along with your passionate, possessive love for your mother, you can hate her when she 'cheats' on you in this way.
>
> Your father might seem to be the one who represents those limits, his presence leading to the 'no'. It is easier to bear if your father is also sympathetic, and harder if he is harsh or humiliating.

That oscillation between frustrated, hostile impulses and dread of damage and punishment can be seen in Klein's work with a little girl whose symptoms of anxiety had begun at 15 months – at the same time as her mother became pregnant with her younger brother (Klein, 1945).

> When seen, at 2 years, 9 months, **Rita** oscillated between signs of hatred and suspicion of her mother, possessiveness and suspicion of her father, and anxious clinging. Her mother was described as neurotic and obviously ambivalent to her daughter. Rita slept in her parents' bedroom and would have had some awareness of her parents' sexual activity.
>
> Rita needed to be tucked in tightly at night for fear that a mouse or a 'butzen' might come in the window and bite off her 'butzen'. She tucked her dolls in equally tightly. Her play was inhibited. She would repetitively clean her dolls and change their clothes. Sometimes Rita cruelly told her dolls off: then she would cling fearfully to her mother, asking, 'Am I good? Do you love me?'

Klein commented in a matter-of-fact way on the little girl's games, and the anxieties that lay behind them. She spoke of Rita's loving feelings, but also her greedy, possessive and hostile ones. So, in one session,

> *Rita put an elephant by her doll's pillow, saying that if she did not do so 'the child would steal into its parents' bedroom and either do them some harm or take something away from them'.*
>
> Klein said that Rita wanted to attack her parents but that she also (the elephant, and helped by an elephant-father) wanted to protect them.
>
> In a later session Rita played a game in which *she was going by cab with her teddy bear to a 'good' woman with whom they were going to have 'a marvellous time'. She got rid of the engine driver and took his place. But he kept returning, wanting to claim the teddy bear.*
>
> Klein interpreted that Rita wanted to get rid of her engine driver/father and take his place, having a *marvellous time* with her mother. She wanted to take her father's teddy bear (his penis and all that it represented) so that she had something exciting and good to offer her mother.

Rita was helped, not by a change in external circumstances, but by having her hating feelings understood as well as her loving ones towards her parents. Now less attacked by Rita's hidden wishes, they were felt by her to be less attacking.

> Rita became more relaxed with her mother, and affectionate with her father and baby brother. She kissed and hugged her bear saying, *'I'm not a bit unhappy anymore because I've got such a dear little baby'*
>
> (Klein, 1945, p. 26).

Nature

Klein noted her mother's ambivalence to Rita, the provocation of sharing her parents' bedroom and of the new baby.

But, like Freud, Klein also emphasized what was internal: the part played by the infant's inevitable conflicting feelings of frustration, hostility and of envy. She pointed out that some children are constitutionally more predisposed to difficulty: some children struggle in circumstances which others manage well, and others do surprisingly well in emotionally poor circumstances. Later neonatal studies confirm this view (Stern, 1985; Brazelton & Cramer, 1991).

Some babies really are more difficult than others: they are more reactive and less easily soothed; they disturb more easily from sleep and hate having their clothes removed (Pretorious, 2010).

Stresses faced by the mother while the baby is *in utero*, as well as drugs or medications that affect her heart rate and the neuro-chemicals that cross the placenta play a part. Birth trauma and minor injury have an impact. An infant born significantly premature, with an immature neurological development, is more vulnerable. One who has suffered lack of nutrition in the womb (through placental insufficiency, being a smaller twin, or as a result of being significantly post-mature) is less easily soothed. Genes play some part (Pretorious, 2010).

That baby constitutionally has fewer resources within him to calm himself. He quickly loses a sense of any good care to offset his experience of the terrifyingly bad. His mother, exhausted, may be guiltily aware of feelings of frustration and hatred for her baby who cannot easily be soothed. She is more likely to become depressed (Murray, 1992, 2009). The baby, picking up any of his mother's frustration and depression, will feel in even more of a panic, in a vicious spiral. When his mother's exhausted fury is offset by other moments where she can be warmly, enjoyably involved with him, then she might be unpredictable, but she is not unreachable.

That infant part persists in us as adults. We can oscillate in a more or less extreme way between these positions: one of wishful excitement and power, of having it all and not really needing anyone, and the painful reality that we do not have it all, that we do still need particular others, loved, envied and attacked as they are.

It is not a single struggle and then over, but one which fluctuates and is ongoing.

Note

1   This early 'mothering' is mostly still done by the mother, a grandmother or child-minder – and sometimes by a father.

Chapter 6

The mother and the environment

*There is no such thing as a baby … if you show me a baby you certainly
show me also someone caring for the baby … one sees a 'nursing couple'*
(Winnicott, 1952, p. 99).

Nurture

Several analysts added to Klein's account of the baby by bringing a particularly
careful attention to how the mother (with the help of the father or partner, and a
supportive environment) is able to help her baby – and the effect on him when
she is less able to do so.

Donald Winnicott (1896–1971)

Donald Winnicott's experience was as a paediatrician working with young
children and their mothers, as well as an analyst.

He describes how, when all goes well in the earliest days of her infant's life,
the mother attunes herself sensitively to her baby, allowing him the illusion that
he is still merged with her. The baby does not need his mother to be perfect but
'good enough' (Winnicott, 1953, 1964). Then, slowly, and in response to the
baby's growing capacity, she allows more space between herself and him: she
gently disillusions him.

A baby learns who he (or she) is, mirrored through his parents' eyes. There is
an aggression that is necessary, life-giving as the baby sucks lustily, heedlessly
at the bottle or the breast. This is separate from the baby's feelings of hate when
he is frustrated, and when he envies his mother her goods. Many babies have an
attachment to a soft toy (or blanket): one which can represent the mother but
that is not her, one who can be loved and clung to – and also safely hated,
beaten up and abandoned (1953).

The baby needs his mother and her love for him (and his father's) to survive
his attacks on her: his greedy, loving ones and his frustrated and envious ones. If he
feels too guilty and fears that his loving feelings are insufficient, or are not noticed,

his capacity for hopeful, rambunctious play is inhibited. The more support his mother has in this tough task from a partner, family or friends, the better (1945).

Winnicott points out how a mother, who for her own needs wants to be a perfect mother with a perfect, responsive baby, can hate her baby when he is not – and when he is more separate from her. If she cannot tolerate her hateful feelings, she might express them in being neglectful of, or intrusive with, her baby (1960). The child is more likely to fit in with a self that is false, rather than have the space and the un-intrusive support to find out who he is.

He described a series of consultations with a 1-year-old, who had suffered increasingly severe episodes of fitting following a bad case of gastro-enteritis at six months (1971).

> He took the 1-year-old on his knee, where she sat listlessly while he spoke with her mother. After a while she furtively bit his knuckle. When Winnicott did not react, the toddler bit his knuckle several more times and threw a wooden spatula he gave her on the floor.
>
> A couple of days later, again on his knee, the 1-year-old bit his knuckle – but this time without showing any guilt. She became more lively, biting and throwing away the spatula. Then, for the first time, she began to play with her toes. Her fitting stopped.

We cannot be precisely sure how this sensitive analyst/paediatrician was able to help so quickly. But presumably, in his holding of the toddler, his response to her and her bite, what he conveyed was that curious, biting and attacking feelings (which might have been linked in the baby's and in the mother's mind to the attack of gastro-enteritis) were acceptable and would not do intolerable damage.

Anna Freud (1895–1982)

> *In reality, it is not the absence of irrational emotional attachments which helps a child to grow up normally but the painful and often disturbing process of learning how to deal with such emotions*
> (Freud, A. & Burlingham, 1974[1944], p. 594).

As a result of her experience of young children from impoverished families in a nursery in Vienna, and in children separated from parents in residential War Nurseries in London, analyst Anna Freud gained a wealth of clinical research experience of babies and young children when their development was normal and when, sadly, it was not.

She detailed the birth of the mind out of the body and the infant's making sense of himself in relation to his mother (1954). She described how, bodily, the baby or young child needs to be handled: he needs to feel that he is possessed by his mother. He is happily, safely, aroused by his mother's interest and her pleasure in him in an emotional, responsive dance, but when this is punitive or negligent, the baby can turn to auto-erotism, aggression or head-banging.

By the second year of life, the toddler 'can safely be said (to) love his mother … but he is insatiable and rivals his sibs and his father for his mother's affection. His mother is recognized as whole, separate from himself: both hated and loved' (Freud, A. & Burlingham, 1944, p. 181).

But not all children make this developmental step. Bearing conflicting feelings of love and hate is an achievement, based on a sense of a reliable maternal figure. Some children had little capacity to notice or label feelings, which were shut down or discharged elsewhere.

In the absence of their mothers in the War Nursery, though better fed and clothed, the youngsters were emotionally cut off or volatile, doing poorly in tasks such as toilet training and language development. Putting them into small family groups with a stable mothering figure helped them to settle (Freud, A. & Burlingham, 1944).[1]

Anna Freud argued that aggression can be a response to experience of parenting which is punitive or is negligent: then, the child identifies with the adult's aggression and turns it outwards on to others (as seen in many children's games), or inwards on to himself, as useless and worthless (Freud, A. & Burlingham, 1944).

She gave a moving example of the emotional rescue of a little boy, **Tony**, who came into the Nursery aged 2 years 9 months (Freud, A. & Burlingham, 1944, pp. 240–243; Edgcumbe, 2000, pp. 25–31).

Since he was 8 months, Tony's father had been away in the war. Age 2, his mother had gone into a Sanatorium for TB and Tony had been in a series of foster homes. He did what he was told and was no trouble to anyone – but he showed no emotion.

Tony was unreachable in his flat, forlorn affect. What helped were two episodes of illness when he spent time cuddled in his nurse, Mary's, lap: on the second occasion he was isolated in the sick room with her for several weeks, with scarlet fever.

Tony began to bond with Mary and as a result of this, he became passionately demanding: fearful of losing her and accusing her of misdeeds. At bedtime he would angrily send her away – and then want her back. His passionate demands and protest was a result of having some fledgling hope in the reliability of his substitute mother figure.

Tony's demands were hard for Mary and for the Nursery to bear, but were the beginning of him becoming more emotionally alive. Gradually he became more settled. He could play while Mary got on with her work, as long as he knew where she was and that he could go to her when he needed.

There were some serious setbacks, including when his father came to tell him that his mother had died. Tony became quiet and withdrawn. He told Mary 'my daddy chucked a big stone at me and I cried, and I do not like my daddy any more and I will never like him again' – though he still liked to hear Mary's stories of his father.

He began to lose precious possessions, common to children who feel themselves to be lost (Freud, A., 1967). But still, after a time, he could tell Mary his sad news and begin to grieve.

Most of us are lucky enough not to have suffered the disruption and losses that Tony did. Even so, difficulties early on can have a subtle but profound impact on later life.

These analytically based findings are corroborated by later studies of infants' attachment behaviour.[2]

Attachment

A parent's capacity to be emotionally responsive to the baby is vital to the baby's sense of security, in relating to himself and to others.

When 18-month-old babies are left temporarily by their mother with a stranger in a strange room, on her return they show characteristic patterns of response.

Some, the *securely attached* go to their mother, crying and protesting. They are able to be comforted by their mother and in time can be put down and can explore once more. Other toddlers cling and cry but cannot be comforted and will not tolerate being put down again. (An *insecure attachment*.) Some others show a *detached* style: not going to their mother for comfort (or to protest) on her return but turning away, grizzling and exploring only half-heartedly. A final group show *disorganized* patterns: of conflict between longing for comfort and avoidance and fear, which they manage by *dissociating*

(Ainsworth et al., 1971).

The toddler's pattern of attachment is heavily determined by the mother's ability to sensitively cue in to her baby (and separately by the father's capacity to do so). This capacity can be predicted before the baby's birth, by the parents' capacity to talk of their own childhood realistically and without idealisation (Steele et al., 2010).

Some parents, who could acknowledge past neglect or abuse and had come to some terms with it, were able to be emotionally aware of their baby's cues. Others, who had managed earlier difficulty by pushing it from mind, were less responsive: they were likely to be over-anxious and intrusive, or to shut down and block out their baby's cues.

In this way, that impact, undigested, could pass on wordlessly, trans-generationally, to their infant.

The baby in the parent's mind

Even before her baby is born, a mother and father have their own idea of the baby they expect him (or her) to be.

They may hope that he will be a perfect, loving baby to make up for disappointments earlier on – and find it hard when he protests and will not be satisfied and when he loves and enjoys others, too. Some parents are able to attune more easily to a quieter, withdrawn baby and find a lively, demanding baby too much. Others feel rejected by a withdrawn baby and enjoy the reassuring neediness of an infant who is more responsive and demanding.

A parent who had a particular loss or difficulty in childhood, such as the death of a sibling or the illness of a parent, can respond to their baby as if he were that figure from the past – one who is angry, critical or enviable – rather than being able to see their new baby for who he (or she) is (Fraiberg et al., 1980; Barrows, 1999).[3] A parent may particularly hope for a boy or a girl – and may find it hard to accommodate to a baby who is the 'wrong' gender.

A mother who is depressed is not able to respond in a lively way to her child (Murray et al., 1996) and child development studies have noted the distressing impact on a baby when, even for a short time, the mother is asked to maintain an impassive face, and how quickly the baby will give up and turn away (Tronick et al., 1978).

When a parent is less able to notice their baby as his own separate person, not the one of their wishful fantasy, then it is confusing for the baby, who has to fit in or feel that somehow he is not right.

It is the combination of a sensitive baby and parents with less capacity to be attuned which can lead to significant emotional and behavioural difficulties (Murray et al., 1996).

The impact on neurological development

Responsive help, or its lack, affects the baby in his physiological and neurological development. Genetically based neurological development continues through the first year of life. Particularly when he is genetically vulnerable, the baby is helped by a responsive environment, by feelings of trust and safety (Pretorius, 2010).

A carer who is able to attend to and repair emotional ruptures helps regulate the infant's arousal levels (Schore, 2010, p. 30, 2011). When the baby's stress levels are chronically high, he suffers structural changes in the brain, hippo-campal atrophy and synaptic loss (Bremner, 2005). Then, he will be less able to pay attention or use verbal encoding in which to think or to remember. Instead, he dissociates (Yovell et al., 2015).

A baby observed

The following is an account of a baby, observed weekly in the first year of his life, who had some capacity to remain robust even in the face of considerable difficulties.

> **Jamie** was Franny's first baby. Franny's father, to whom she had been very close, had recently died. She had a more difficult relationship with her

mother and spoke of wanting to be a better mother to Jamie than she felt her own mother had been to her.

In the first few weeks after Jamie's birth, Franny would sit in bed, her baby propped against her knees, the two gazing at each other. Jamie slept in his parents' bed.

Work demands made Franny's partner, Steve, frequently absent and unavailable. But emotional factors might have played their part, too: Steve had been given up for adoption as a baby, and he had missed out on his birth-mother's care. As well as wanting the best for his young son, it must have been disturbing for him seeing Jamie get the loving attention from his mother that Steve had not had from his.

Franny's mother stayed for two weeks after the birth. When she left, Franny was isolated. She could not bear to leave Jamie for a moment, even to get herself a drink or have a bath. Franny became exhausted and then increasingly depressed. In the background, unspoken, must have been Franny's mourning for her loved father, who had never got to see her baby son. She sadly thought that Jamie must find her a 'boring old Mummy'.

In an effort to be more lively, Franny would rather shrilly rattle toys in front of Jamie's face and he would become increasingly agitated. Franny seemed subtly neglectful of Jamie. She put few covers on Jamie when he slept: he had difficulties settling to sleep and would rouse easily. She was slow to notice his early signs of hunger and only when he was increasingly fractious did she prepare milk for the bottle and let it cool. Some babies would have been in such distress by the time the bottle arrived that they could no longer take it – but Jamie still accepted the bottle with relief and some vigour.

Franny's depression worsened: she returned to work part-time and did not notice the impact it had on Jamie. A crisis happened when Jamie was 6 months old: Steve planned to be away one long weekend with his sports team and Franny was furious. She agreed to cover a work emergency, leaving Jamie with a new young babysitter. (Was Franny abandoning Jamie, rather as she felt abandoned by Steve – and, behind him, by her father, who had so recently died?)

That day, Jamie was observed on the babysitter's lap, listlessly allowing himself to be fed, muscles limp, and staring into the middle distance as if he had just given up. It was painful to witness.

And then things began to settle. Franny found a child-minder who was warm and with whom Jamie settled well. She found a friend with a baby of the same age and with whom she could share the inevitable frustrations and resentments in mothering.

Franny was able to demand more of Steve. He became more involved in Jamie's care – and was amazed that his son responded warmly. He was needed and wanted: not just looking on from the outside.

Franny started to appreciate her mother's visits and support: she was more forgiving of her mother's failings now that she discovered that mothering a young baby was not as easy as she had assumed.

Jamie became more settled but he was still sensitive. At 9 months he was playful in his mother's arms and reached out for her earring: Franny reacted with alarm. Jamie instantly became tense and looked away. Franny calmed down and was able to reassure him.

At 15 months Jamie seemed to be a lively toddler, whacking the sofa with a ruler that belonged to his father and going to his mother for reassurance and warm interchanges. She commented how Jamie 'loves his old Mum'.

Jamie's constitution enabled him to tolerate his mother's intrusions and allowed him to make use of all that his mother, however imperfectly, was able to offer. This then had the happy result of reassuring Franny that she was doing a 'good enough' job.

Jamie's capacity may have been enhanced by the care and devotion his mother had offered him in the first few weeks of his life – and which then contributed to some primitive bedrock experience that somewhere there was something good and safe to hold on to. But it was evident that Frannie's difficulties, including the recent loss of her father and the withdrawal of her partner in the early months, had affected how she perceived and responded to her son – and the impact it had on Jamie, seen especially at 6 and 9 months.

Might there be a lingering impact of these early months? Might Jamie in certain circumstances, such as being alone too long, re-experience those feelings of his despairing 6-month-old state? If so, he would not remember consciously what it was that seemed familiar and bleak. Someone close to him might notice him slipping away emotionally, but logically it would make little sense.

(In an analysis, such noticing of a shift of mood brought in the room [in the transference], and finding words to convey it, might allow more conscious access to what otherwise remains nameless, invisible.)

Other babies are not as lucky as Jamie. They have less tolerance of frustration and may be too agitated to accept the delayed feed. A depressed mother may have fewer resources, within or outside herself. A father may be absent or with far fewer resources to help.

Then the baby has to manage much more difficulty. He turns to more primitive and chronic mechanisms of shutting down and turning away. This is the emotional territory of which Bion speaks (as I describe in the next chapter).

Notes

1 Parents were encouraged to keep contact as much as possible and after the Nursery's evacuation to the countryside, a monthly bus was hired to bring them out to visit.
2 In 1942, Melanie Klein and Anna Freud agreed to meet up privately with a small group of followers to discuss their clinical findings and theoretical differences. Others

thought that this should take place within the Society as a whole. Sadly, in that larger group format, the mood became antagonistic, ending in a decision that the two analysts would run separate trainings. Much of Anna Freud's research findings were published in a separate journal (Young-Bruehl, 2008). A middle group of analysts found much to value in both camps. Klein and Anna Freud continued to read and respond to each other's writing (Holder, 2005).

3 Making these associations with the past conscious is often extremely helpful to new parents. Sadly, many parent–infant programmes which do such work are under threat of cuts.

Part II

Freedom of thought

Freedom of thought – and at best I think we still have a very limited freedom in that respect – means the freedom to know our own thoughts and that means knowing the unwelcome as well as the welcome, the anxious thoughts, those felt as "bad" or "mad", as well as constructive thoughts and those felt as "good" or "sane" ...

(Segal, 1981[1977])

In this next section, I move aside from describing the ongoing development of the young child to look at some of the unacceptable feelings that are so disturbing, so *rough* and *beastly* against which we set up protective barriers.

Freedom of thought, as described above, might look as if it should be easy, at least the bit about the good and the sane. But knowing about the mad, the bad and the sad in a way that really touches you is much harder. It is very easy then to slip away and return to a more dubious relationship with reality: that wishing should make it so.

Chapter 7

The mad

Turning and turning in the widening gyre
The falcon cannot hear the falconer;
Things fall apart; the centre cannot hold;
Mere anarchy is loosed upon the world . . .
(Yeats, 2000, 'The Second Coming')

Analyst **Wilfred Bion** (1897–1979) brought his experiences (as an officer in a tank regiment during the chaos of the First World War, an army psychiatrist with shell-shocked soldiers, and in analysing some very disturbed adult patients) to understanding those primitive states which can continue on through life.

Bion articulated how, when under the sway of discomfort, the infant bears primitive, panicky experiences. His sensations, since not yet named, are literally unthinkable. They are felt as bad, toxic and, without help, the only way to manage them is to fragment them somehow (split them) and get rid of them from mind (project them).

A mother (or father) who can bear to notice her infant's distress, without feeling too panicked herself, can manage it in her mind like emotional digestion. She holds him, *contains* him, emotionally as well as physically (Bion, 1962). She conveys her belief that all is not a disaster. She offers words in which to think. He discovers strategies to soothe himself even in his mother's absence.

But a mother, for her own reasons, might not be able to hear her baby as the person that he is, separate from her. She might have difficulties that stem from her own experience of being parented herself; she might be depressed; she might be parenting alone, or with a partner who is unsupportive. Her baby's disturbance and complaints can feel intolerable – an accusation that she is no good – and she will want to manage her own distress by making her baby stop, or by shutting down herself.

The baby who is less emotionally contained has to manage feelings which do not make sense and which dangerously threaten to overwhelm him – and his carer, too. He is left with his fragmented feelings, extreme and dangerous, which he has not been able to bring together in any safe, meaningful way.

The baby can shut down, or simply not develop, a part of his mind that has any curiosity about knowing himself, that can think or make connections. A hard shell is constructed around what otherwise feels too soft and vulnerable. Turning to action can be an attempt to rid himself of such unwanted experience. It is not the same as florid psychosis, but even so, reality has become distorted.

That baby, as he grows, may have an idea that *something* is wrong but have little idea what, and little hope that there is anything or anyone to help. Any offer of help to connect with that part of his mind can then seem too alarming and to be avoided at all cost.

Turning and turning

Most of us can have a part of our mind that is 'mad', in that we are not able to fully register external reality as a result of what we have got rid of: pockets of our mind, which, under pressure, can become no-go areas, fiercely defended and hard to access (Tustin, 1986).

In emptying out of mind what feels too threatening, we also empty out much of what is important – including the awareness of not-always-comfortable reality. It can leave us feeling bleak, because of what we have got rid of: puzzled, because it is no longer clear what is ours, or what is out there. It leaves us without the resources to feel we can know ourselves much – and then without the tools to connect with anyone else. We might be left feeling extremely calm, but remote or fiercely in the right, convinced and brooking no other point of view.

That state of mind is maddening, since we may well have the puzzling feeling that something is not quite right, but cannot put our finger on it. It's maddening for others, too. Lurking is a sense of panic, blame and confusion.

> While able to function in an intellectual job, emotionally **Lara** was in a frenzy, and with little sense of having a mind to help her. She longed to have a stable relationship and children, but something always went wrong. She was in despair.
>
> When Lara was a baby, her mother had been very depressed. Growing up, Lara felt a background sense of panic always looming. She would clutch at friends, and later boyfriends, wanting them to make everything better and then being disappointed and critical of them for failing or devastated when they rejected her because of the pressure she put on them. If a boyfriend continued to be interested in her, Lara would think there must be something wrong with him.
>
> As she settled into her analysis, Lara began to feel that something of her panic was noticed and offered back to her in a way that she could begin to tolerate. She recognized how she could inflame her feelings since this kept everyone close.
>
> What also became apparent (in the transference relation with her male analyst) was not only how sensitive Lara was to any lapse in her analyst's

perfect attention, but when he *was* attentive and really touched her emotionally, how alarmed she felt. Then she would find fault and push him away.

It was as if it was safer to have her analyst predictably unreliable than being helpful and valued. If she valued him, she might be vulnerable to missing him in his absence; she might feel envious of his capacity. In her analysis, this could be slowly unpicked.

Initially, Lara felt in a panic; she raged at her analyst, complaining that he was blaming her. As he remained patient but did not back down, Lara began reluctantly to consider what he was telling her. She could see how she pushed aside what he offered. This was a come-down for her – but it was also reassuring: her analyst might not be as useless as she had assumed.

Lara began to wonder whether her mother might have offered her more that she had not been able to make use of, and in that way she had possibly added to her mother's frantic distress. This was a very painful thought for her. Even so, putting it into words and thinking about it consciously meant that Lara was less in need of reassurance for a dread that was otherwise unthinkable.

Lara began to see a different version of her mother: not one who was only 'useless' and 'bad'. She could see how depressed and frantic her mother had been, for understandable, if very sad, reasons. It was upsetting to think about her mother's difficulties and the impact it had had on her, but her world felt softer and safer.

Lara felt that she could have memories of a mother who was loving, despite her real difficulties. As she did so, she felt she had inside her a good, though not perfect, mother and a greater capacity to mother herself: she had a stronger sense of someone helpful internally.

Then Lara met someone. She could see that he had his flaws, but strengths too. She noticed that she could envy him his strengths, since this made her feel rivalrous and inadequate. Being consciously aware of this meant that she was more able to resist the impulse to rubbish him, as she had previous boyfriends.

She was more able to have a mind to think and to notice – her anxious and hostile impulses as well as her more appreciative ones.

The falcon cannot hear the falconer

When feelings such as a longing for connection and help feel too dangerous, we can lodge them in someone else and become a good carer of the need, which is now all out there, in them (and rather despised by us). But if our own needs cannot be noticed or communicated, then we are likely to find ourselves increasingly depleted.

When we manage what is painful by pushing it from mind, then we have little way of hearing ourselves:

Meena was apparently untroubled with few needs. She seemed cheerful, but remote. Others were concerned, but not her.

When Meena was small, her mother had to work three jobs for the family to get by. Her elder sister, at 7, looked after the younger siblings and cooked the evening meal for the family until their parents returned from work. Meena's parents were doing their best to care for their children, but there were so many demands on them.

At 4, Meena had a habit of going off and getting lost. When her parents took to locking the doors to keep her in, she would climb out the window, with a sense of excitement. She would eat little that was offered her and got pleasure in secretly pouring the milk her mother gave her down the drain. In school, she could not bear to ask for help, and failed many exams as a result. It seemed as if, in this way at least, she was in control of her deprivation and any sense of desperate worry and longing was in her parents.

In her analysis, too, Meena would 'get lost'. Sometimes literally so, and she would not come in to her analytic session but (she later revealed) would remain secretly outside her analyst's house. Her analyst was concerned but, apparently, not Meena. It was as if feeling herself to have an appetite or emotional need left her frighteningly vulnerable. This began to be explored in her analysis.

For the first time, Meena began to notice painful feelings of missing her mother when she was away on long trips, visiting family. She could be more concerned for herself. She found herself more open, and closer to those in her family.

Things fall apart

When feeling lost, in a panic or shut down, fight or flight can at least seem to offer a possibility of finding some aliveness, some connection, however frustrating.

You might career from one row to another, one affair to another, one hectic activity to another. Others may want and wait for you, but you won't them. Others might feel little and small, but not you. You can fight your corner – but somewhere have an uneasy feeling that the fight could be more about keeping others at bay.

It is hard to believe that others will love you of their own free will; rather, that you have to manipulate them through charm, bullying, your successes or through frantic helplessness (in which case their attention is not that reassuring). You can turn to hatred and blame. It is hard then to know who you really are, or if anything at all is reliable or real. It can be very painful to face what has gone wrong in the past, and it is an act of courage to do so.

Sinead presented in a frantic manner, always on the go, barely able to slow down. She had a responsible job and was doing her best to mother her children. At the same time she moved house several times, was running up debts, and using drink and casual sex to medicate herself.

As Sinead slowly settled in the analysis, what emerged were vague memories of sexual abuse by her father and others. She was not sure what was real or not. Gradually, she pieced things together.

There was a history of family abuse that went back several generations. A cousin and an aunt had both complained of abuse, and had been ignored and ridiculed.

Sinead spoke of her memories with her mother. At first, her mother seemed to confirm Sinead's ideas and suggested that as a child she, too, had been a victim of abuse. Then she clammed up. The family argued that she should not bring it up when her father was old and unwell.

But Sinead stayed clear in her own mind. She made a complaint to the police. She told a few trusted friends and colleagues. She lost touch with her family and she felt lonely.

Still she felt proud that she had faced up to a painful truth. It was not easy for her but, in doing so, Sinead felt more settled. She no longer had to keep in constant motion to hold something unbearable at bay. She was able to treat herself with more care.

The centre cannot hold

An example of emptying out links within his mind is Freud's patient, the **Wolf Man** (whose wolf dream was described earlier) (Freud, 1918).[1]

Twenty-three-year-old Russian, Sergei Panchikoff, had come to Freud suffering from symptoms of depression, suspicion and feeling not *quite alive*. He was physically constipated and needed daily enemas.

The year before coming to Freud, his sister had killed herself, followed some months later by his father. He expressed pleasure that he would not have to share the family wealth.[2] He was helped by Freud's analysis of his wolf dream: he was able to return to Russia, marry and work.

During the Russian Revolution, Sergei Panchikoff lost all his lands. He returned to Vienna, gaining considerable attention as Freud's famous patient, the Wolf Man. By that time Freud had been operated on for oral cancer, was looking frail and had a prosthesis in his jaw. Freud arranged a collection to help his now impoverished former patient.

He had renewed symptoms – of constipation and a delusional belief that he had a hole in his nose. He went into treatment with another analyst, who took up his excited hostile feelings towards Freud (Mack Brunswick, 1928). So he said of an ill doctor, whom he associated with Freud:

'how agreeable it is that I, the patient, am really healthy, whereas he, the
doctor, has a serious illness', and when that doctor died:
    'My God! Now I can't kill him any more!'

Sergei Panchikoff seemed to have managed any feelings, including sadness or
guilt, in relation to the suicides of his sister and father, or towards his former
analyst, now frail and ill, by expunging them. (And behind that, too, all the
family circumstances which had driven both his sister and his father to kill
themselves.)

Instead, he filled himself up with excitement and triumph. He got rid of
anything emotionally *stuck* and *shitty* inside himself through his daily
enemas, though this left him anxious, suspicious of being cheated and
delusional about the 'hole' in his nose: no longer a mental hole but instead
a physical one.

Noticing a mental hole might mean noticing who and what had been emptied
from his mind: his fears of his rage and damage to anyone he might once have
loved and needed. It would mean becoming painfully aware of his emotional
deprivation in the middle of such material wealth – in some part contributed to
by him.

Finding words that have meaning, memories that can be held in mind,
can make a great difference even if it doesn't make pain and difficulty go
away.

Analyst Paul Williams wrote vividly of his own disturbing, abusive family
life and his experience of being emotionally *pulverized*. Looking back, he could
describe his mind as a *jellyfish* as a result of, but also a way of managing, what
was intolerable (Williams, 2012).

*You don't ask an injured fox how it feels to have been crushed under the
wheels of a truck do you? Cracked limbs cloud eyes jaw-dropping blood
bile asphalt tell the story. So it is with children crusher works on plastic
unformed jellyfish mind muscle cramps incontinence night terrors asthma
nervous spasms seizures sickness …*

But it was only with his analyst, registering the impact, finding words, that he
could begin to develop a mind which might hold on to himself, and his
experience.

It is not easy feeling disturbed: noticing what is shameful, how we may be
fearful, what it is that leaves us feeling little and vulnerable. But if not, there
is little room for thinking, curiosity and for feeling grounded. If we can
survive, keep on thinking, and still hold on to sympathy for that *us* who
is firing off all our cannons, then with luck we may find that not all has been
lost.

When reality – imperfection, difference, separateness and loss – is infuriating but not a complete disaster, then we are more open to painful
experience, the *bad* and the *sad*, but also more open to those of love and
pleasure.

Notes

1 Page 11.
2 There is a much fuller description of the Wolf Man in Appendix E.

Chapter 8

The bad

The beast in me
Is caged by frail and fragile bars
Restless by day
And by night rants and rages at the stars
God help the beast in me
(Nick Lowe, 1994)

We have feelings that we would rather we did not, which are shameful, conflictual and are painful to notice. Their source is often primitive, passionate feelings from infancy, which may have been suppressed but have not gone away. Ones that are a result of inevitable frustrations, of having to wait too long, of not being in control of *everything*, and of the pain of separateness, dependence and exclusion.

For those who are luckier, such frustrations are built on a bedrock of being noticed and included at least some of the time; protest and rage can be tolerated without collapse or retaliation – even if it doesn't lead to getting the *all* that we may wish.

But, for others, this emotional grounding is less robust. A parent who is depressed or overwhelmed is not able to be emotionally responsive; a mother or father who is fragile might find their baby's protest too hurtful and withdraw, collapse or lash out. Without such moments of reassuring lively contact, there is no safe space for the baby's angry frustration and demands as a part of a passionate interchange.

Feelings of deprivation, rage and revenge can spiral. Knowing of such hostile feelings makes us hateful to ourselves and, we will fear, to those we also love. Then we may attempt to suppress such unacceptable feelings, or turn to justification and provocation to prove that it is the other who is the one so unforgivably bad.

However much, at a rational level, we have accepted frustrating reality, even so, barely under the surface, some of that underlying intensity still remains, although unacknowledged in adult life. Such a struggle between loving feelings and hateful ones is an inevitable part of our human condition, however responsive the environment. There is a bit of most of us in the following example.

Pete was a sensitive baby; he was wanted, his parents were together: it wasn't perfect, but it was okay.

He took badly the return of his father from working away when he was 3, and the arrival of a new baby. It felt intolerable to see the pleasure on his mother's face with her new baby, and not him. He was angry and difficult. His parents were sympathetic but thought he would get over it in time. But Pete didn't want to allow his parents to make him feel better – since this would mean accepting a reality that was just *not fair*.

As he grew up Pete withdrew, feeling critical and aggrieved. His parents felt helpless, then exasperated – and they pulled away from him. He longed to be reassured of his parents' love for him, but he felt this made him pathetic and he sneered at such feelings.

Pete had got rid of (projected) his painful feelings of being left out and unwanted by his parents after the arrival of the next baby: instead he made them the unwanted ones. This made him feel powerful, rather than miserable and left out, but it left him deprived of his love and need for his mother, and for his father, too. He no longer knew that he wanted anything from them.

He feared being unlovable since his parents had not fought for him more – but also, painfully, because, somewhere out of conscious sight, he knew that he had done damage to those he had once loved: his mother, and his father too.

Hatred and envy can seem so disturbing when we have pushed such unacceptable feelings far from mind. Part of the satisfaction in seeing such feelings portrayed for us, safely *out there* in books or in drama, is an uneasy recognition of them in ourselves. So, for example,

- **Iago** envies the successful war hero, Othello, and his happiness in his new marriage. Iago turns feelings of being left out, less loved and admired, to ones of power over Othello by convincing him that his young wife is unfaithful. Othello then is the one who feels small and humiliated. Othello kills Desdemona and then himself. Iago, meanwhile, is triumphant in his power to spoil the happiness of others, which he does not share.
- **Hedda Gabler** cannot bear that her ex-lover, writer Lovberg, has overcome his alcoholism and produced the book he always dreamed of, with the help of his timid but devoted partner – and not her. He will get the professorship and not her husband. Hedda destroys Lovberg's only manuscript and prompts him to shoot himself, complaining when he does not do so *beautifully*. She kills herself.
- In Harry Potter, the orphan Tom Riddle becomes the wicked **Voldemort** who sets out to kill off all that is good and loving, in Harry's mother's love for her son – which is intolerable to him.

We may find such characters shocking, but most of us will recognize, however fleetingly, some of those feelings that are so unacceptable to our conscious mind.

Why would you notice these considerably less than perfect feelings?

Because unrecognized, such feelings can underlie feelings of unease, mistrust and self-hatred. If you half-recognize such feelings as your own, you will assume that you will be attacked in turn. It leaves you guilty, less sure of being lovable – and then even more envious of others who seem happily to take pleasure in what they have.

Refusing to notice any less-than-generous feelings and keeping yourself only *innocent* leaves you less access to your more rational and moral capacities to help. You might fear being found out and punished, but have less capacity to allow care, or to care for others.

The problem of envy

> Blasted with sighs, and surrounded with tears,
> Hither I come to seek the spring,
> And at mine eyes, and at mine ears,
> Receive such balms as else cure every thing.
> *But O ! self-traitor, I do bring*
> *The spider Love, which transubstantiates all,*
> *And can convert manna to gall;*
> *And that this place may thoroughly be thought*
> *True paradise, I have the serpent brought.*
> (John Donne, 'Twicknam Gardens',
>   my emphasis)

It is much easier to acknowledge feelings of protest and hatred in response to frustration and deprivation. It is understandable. The problem of envy is that it attacks what we know to be good (even if not perfect). And that feels so shameful to notice.

When someone has attributes that we admire and value, envy is an almost inevitable part of what we feel. We wish we had those lovely goods for ourselves and may feel frustration and anger at the world, which has not offered it to us, too. Our admiration may stimulate us to work to gain those attributes for ourselves, though reality will inevitably remind us that we cannot be the best and have it all, even some of the time.

One way to manage awareness of envy of what is good and is not ours is by diminishing what the other has. Manna is turned to gall. Then there is nothing left to envy. *I didn't want it anyway!* But in doing so, we are less able to feel happily hungry for them and what they have to offer.

In Donne's poem above, with a heavy heart the poet is recognising his very mixed feelings at his friend's good fortune, his paradise. He is disgusted by his *spider love*. He recognizes that it is spoiling both his friend's pleasure and the possibility of his sharing in his friend's manna. But he still, painfully, feels it.

Envy can make it harder to freely take pleasure in what we have, for having anything openly pleasurable means that it may be snatched or spoiled in turn.

> Consciously, **Ron** didn't feel excluded by his parents' close relationship, for he believed himself to be the preferred partner of each of them. He secretly knew of his envy of his successful elder brother, but he had always seen himself as the charming sociable one.
>
> Years later and married, while his brother was single, in some part of his mind Ron feared that his brother's singleness was due to the damage done by his quietly rivalrous attacks on him. Ron did not feel he could take too much pleasure in what he had, for he believed it would be bitterly resented by his brother – much as he resented his brother for his professional success.
>
> He could not allow himself whole-heartedly to enjoy his relation with his partner, because this might be noticed and envied. He could not enjoy his creative work because this would be seen as having *too much*, and he would be punished.
>
> Ron had got rid of his awareness of his painful feelings of envy, but at the cost of being inhibited by what felt like others' envy of him.

When the environment is less good, frustration, hatred, envy and jealousy all increase. Early loss and neglect can make difficulties much worse.

> As a baby, **Marian** was given up for adoption by her young, unmarried mother. For the first eighteen months she lived with several different foster parents. She shut down so much that there was concern that she might be deaf.
>
> Her adoptive mother, who longed for a baby of her own, found Marian's lack of responsiveness hurtful. It seemed that she responded with more effort, then with increasing frustration – and finally cruelty. Then she would weep with guilt and shame.
>
> Marian would feel excited at this. She was powerful not helpless. She had proved her adoptive mother to be stupid and worthless, not lovable, not someone who would matter if she was lost (as she had already lost several other mothers). This way of relating became more mutually entrenched and cruel. Her father withdrew.
>
> In her anxious wish to reach out to this remote little girl, Marian's mother might well have been intrusive. But had she given up and with-drawn, Marian would likely have stayed lost. Sadly, there was not the psychotherapy support that might have helped them.[1]

In her analysis, Marian wanted to feel perfectly wanted by the perfect analyst: this, she hoped, would address all past wrong. At first it did feel perfect: she felt noticed, acknowledged, sympathised with.

And then, inevitably, it wasn't: there were payments to be made, sessions that came to an end, and breaks that felt abandoning and infuriating. Marian so longed that her analyst would just want her and nothing, no one else – and she didn't.

Her analyst spoke of this and Marian was relieved that some of her possessive rage could be noticed. But it was not only a relief, for it meant that her analyst had an emotional capacity that Marian did not have, and had missed out on. She felt overwhelmed with envy. She had many thoughts of attacking her analyst, including putting burning twigs and faeces through her letterbox. This made her miserably ashamed – and excited.

Marian put increasing pressure on her analyst. She stopped paying her analyst's fees and turned up with new clothes. The analyst spoke of how she now was the one made deprived and helpless, and Marian felt herself to be powerful and withholding. Marian was torn between guilt and glee. Still she did not pay.

Finally, after several months, her analyst reduced the frequency of her sessions until the backlog of her debt was paid.

Marian was outraged. The tension and recrimination grew. (You could say that Marian had provoked her analyst and made her *cruel*, as she had done with her adoptive mother.)

Given her very difficult experiences early on, and in her later life, Marian needed to bring her feelings of desperate hunger, rage and envy. It was terrifying to notice these feelings since it made her dread that she had been given up as an infant because she was bad. These were the things she and her analyst grappled with, and which constantly risked sabotaging what was available for her.

But was it just the degree of Marian's envy?

At this time the analyst was facing the loss of a close family member and was preoccupied. It is likely that, at some level, Marian, so acutely aware of rejection, noticed this. Her provocation could then be seen as a frantic, if destructive, unconscious attempt to get her analyst to attend to her.

Had her analyst been able to understand and address this, it might have helped Marian, but in her preoccupation, sadly she could not. The analysis, now so stressed, broke down.

It is important to be able to discriminate ways in which someone really is flawed and when envy gets in the way, spoiling what is imperfectly on offer.

Whatever the resources and the difficulties of family, friends, or partner, if we cannot let ourselves notice what they enviably have but can only notice ways in which they let us down, we will feel resentful, deprived and miss out on the possibility of rich experiences. And some of that deprivation may be to do with our difficulties in tolerating what is good but is not ours.

Greed

Fighting for external goods as a way to make up for an internal lack may well not satisfy long term. We can want to fill up a sense of emptiness, rather than out of pleasure: food, drink, drugs, sex, money – but we can't really appreciate them.

> **Evan** came from a deprived background, with a father who had left his depressed mother before he was born. He was desperate to have all that he felt he had missed out on materially (and emotionally) and, with a combination of ruthlessness, graft and preparedness to risk, he succeeded.
>
> Evan had a carapace which protected him from feelings of anxiety and need: he wanted to be powerful and in control. He wanted to please and impress his second wife, Jenny, by providing all kinds of material goods and he was distraught when this left her unsatisfied. She complained that he was not emotionally available.
>
> To be close to Jenny, he would have to let down his guard and Evan dreaded doing that: he would feel too exposed and vulnerable. But if he could not, he feared her leaving him: this made him even more desperate and even more needing to protect himself from hurt, in case she did. And this left the relationship even more sadly impoverished.

Necessary anger

When hateful and envious feelings seem too dangerous, it is possible to inhibit all such feelings – and then have little access to anger, aggression or selfishness, which might be helpful. But without access to angry feelings, then we have little to help in the face of others' demands, and this can be very stressful:

> **Liane** had worked for some years in her small business, with Fred, a difficult, but talented colleague. When she was pleased with her work he was rather critical of her (a bit like her depressed mother had been).
>
> Every so often Fred would threaten to resign: Liane would reassure him of his worth and they would settle back to work. She began to resent him more and more and, because she felt guilty for being angry and feared that his depression somehow was her fault, she would be even nicer to him (like with her mother).
>
> As a result of some psychotherapy, Liane felt able to stand up to Fred and she accepted his threat to resign. She found some younger women who were good at their job and were fun. Fred returned some months later asking for his job back. Liane felt terribly guilty, but said 'no'.

It was something entirely new for her to feel that she could stand up for her own interests – and to feel that (while she was concerned for Fred) she did not have to take full responsibility for his well-being. She had found a way to be a *good mother* to herself.

The negative transference

As a patient in analysis, it can seem that the perfect analyst we need is one who is endlessly sympathetic, ready to agree that badness and blame is all out there. We can hope to be confirmed in a version that we are completely in the right and, to the degree that we have any difficulties, it is only someone else's fault.

The thought is very tempting but it can also be a trap. To maintain this we, the patients, have to remain perfect, grateful and good: there is no room for any version of an us who is messier and rougher. The unstated deal is that the analyst should remain perfect, too: not frustrating or abandoning, not painfully challenging, never preoccupied or just wrong. There can be a strong pressure to maintain this claustrophobic status quo for, if not, there is a likelihood that what will emerge is hated separateness and rage.

It is possible to manage this in familiar ways: we may make complaints, but they are directed not towards the analyst but to others instead. Another way is to go on the offensive, hiding behind a wall of fury and self-justification. It is helpful then if the analyst can stand her ground, not overly guilty or needing us to be *reasonable*, but can feel that, however uncomfortably, there is something in what we bring that needs to be teased out and words found.

Bringing bad feelings – hostile, raging, disparaging, defiant, surly ones – into an analysis can be an important part of finding ourselves more fully. We can have some beginning experience that our hateful feelings might not destroy everything. We are being hateful, but we have not quite lost the analyst's thoughtful attention. Then we may be more able to notice and question for ourselves what goes on in those inflamed states of mind. We develop more of a mind to think of ourselves in relation to others who are separate: not just as we want them to be.

Recognizing bad feelings in us, not only out there, is hard to do, facing us with feelings of guilt and despair. But to the degree that we do so, we have a greater sense of active control: of knowing, and being in the end more at ease with, ourselves, less under permanent fear of the eruption of something *slouching* and *beastly* within.

Note

1 And which is increasingly less available.

Chapter 9

The sad

*Depression and failure are a part of everyday life even the more happy and
successful – I might say especially the more happy and successful: it is the
price you pay for joy and success if they come your way. But the price you
pay for trying to evade failure and depression is ten times worse*

(Bion, 1991, p. 180).

Depression is often confused with sadness – but in fact it is the opposite.

Sadness is about experiencing feelings – of grief, guilt, loss, shame, hatred,
hopelessness – in a lively if painful way. In depression, feelings that are felt as
too distressing are shut down. Everything becomes heavy, hopeless, worthless:
we have no sense of lively desire for anything or anyone; we may complain but
have no capacity for active protest.

> A baby whose mother, for her own reasons, cannot respond to his cues, has
> little experience that his efforts enliven her, that he is worthy of her interest.
> A mother who is struggling with depression simply may not have it in her
> to respond in any sort of unforced way. She might fear that letting her baby
> close will infect him with her despair and will keep him at a distance.
>
> The baby may find ways to attempt to please and enliven her by being
> artificially bright or being very good – but in doing so he becomes attentive
> to her internal state, rather than have her help in learning to be attentive to
> his own.
>
> If his mother responds to his complaints with anger or more despair, then
> the baby can worry that it is his fault: his demands have damaged her. One
> way to feel as close as possible to his mother can be by siding with
> (identifying with) her apparent, harsh view – that he is bad and that it would
> be *stupid* to expect more.

Difficulties early on make later problems harder to manage. Some had a parent
who was depressed or ill, neglectful or abusive; there may have been losses due
to a severe illness or death, or through a bitter family breakdown (Brown et al.,

1986; Pound et al., 1988). Those who had not been emotionally contained as a baby and given help to manage unruly feelings are more vulnerable to traumatic reactions to later stress (Garland, 2002).

Such experiences can set a sad template for later relationships. Any new relationship is heavily burdened with this early, almost instinctive, suspicion, self-doubt and self-protection. The child may learn to find a precarious self-esteem which, as long as things go well, is exciting, but in the face of any disappointment or a pulling away can feel like a terrible abandonment – and that now-adolescent, or adult, can instantly shut down, and turn away (becoming the one who abandons).

> After a family catastrophe when he was little, **Dan**'s mother was hospitalized with depression. When she returned she was emotionally unreliable. He played a repetitive game: *carefully building a city of houses, roads – and then smashing it all up*.
>
> From the outside it looked just destructive: but you might also notice how this sad, neglected young boy was representing the catastrophe, as well as smashing up any sense of hope that his mother would find him again, that being safer than so painfully to long for more.
>
> Dan was doubly abandoned, first by his mother, then by his own smashing. Dan felt somehow that his mother did not care for him enough or she would not have left. He punished life and his mother for failing him, and he punished himself, too.
>
> This pattern continued in Dan's adult life: he had relationships which were important to him but as soon as there was an absence, he would feel abandoned and unwanted – and then he would castigate himself for being so weak as to miss his absent lover. He would pull away, defiantly *not caring*, but also feeling bleak and empty.
>
> Dan hated himself when he could see how he smashed everything up, but he also sneered at himself when he didn't, since it left him foolish and vulnerable.
>
> He wondered whether he might let go of his grievance and hatred for all the real losses and neglect he had suffered: but that, too, would be a loss, having warmed him for so many years. And it would face him with what, however imperfectly, might have been more available for him earlier on, had he not turned away and added to his neglect.

Depression is a part of that extreme, black and white (paranoid–schizoid) state of mind, where someone is disastrously bad. And if it is not the other one who is so completely at fault, then you might notice that you have flaws, too. Then you turn that ferocious condemnation inwards: you now are the one who is *rubbish*.

It is possible to put such thoughts out of mind – and instead suffer physical aches and pains, or an unease which makes no logical sense. You can avoid disappointment by not expecting too much – but it leaves you deprived, and resentful of others who seem more able to reach out and find pleasure from others and from life. You may fear that if that resentful, envious you is seen, neither you nor anyone else will want you.

You may feel sorry for yourself and hopeless, but have squashed anything more lively. You have lost access to useful anger to challenge what you do not like, or to fight for what you do. Any difficult emotion that does break through can stir up scorn at having been so weak as to feel it in the first place.

You may drive yourself on to be good: being selfless or, alternatively, glitteringly successful. You can punish yourself by neglect, depriving yourself of food or sleep – as if only weak people have such human needs. When you end up feeling deprived and exhausted, this then feels like even more proof that you are pathetic. The more you are deprived, the more you resent and envy what others have. And so you hate and punish yourself more, in a vicious spiral.

Depression and anger

In the early days of the First World War, and dreading the loss of his sons, Freud wrote a paper on clinical depression (melancholia) comparing it to mourning a death of a loved one.

In both states there is a terrible loss. In depression, the loss is a rejection or a disappointment from someone otherwise loved. In depression (unlike in mourning), there is a also a catastrophic loss of self-worth – and this does not necessarily resolve with time. As Freud put it: 'In mourning it is the world which has become empty: in melancholia it is the ego itself' (Freud, 1917, p. 246).

What was so startling and revolutionary in this paper (and even now, 100 years later, can be overlooked) was that Freud turned the symptoms inside out and pointed out that what might look like the depressed person's sad *plaint* contains something more hidden: an angry *complaint*.

Disappointment or rejection stirs up earlier losses, such as at weaning. One way of holding on to the one who is rejecting is to side with (*identify* with) them and judge ourself through their critical eyes. Then we are surrounded by critical figures not only outside, but within, too. We have little access to angry feelings, or to robust and warm self-belief, but instead hope for others' sympathy through our sad plaints.

Many struggle with sadness, doubt and depression some of the time – even if they never go to their GP, or take medication. They accept it as an inevitable, if unwelcome part of life: one of the downsides to other ups. Others fall into a pit of such despair that climbing out without medical help is impossible. Some need ongoing medication to manage their mood – though there is still a point in noticing what else is going on inside.

Some have experiences in later life which overwhelm what might otherwise have been sufficient internal resources:

Sarah just had too many deaths to cope with. Her first love, and then her father, died before she was 21. She was resilient, cheery, positive – even if, looking back, she might have been a bit over-anxious to be good as a way of warding off further disaster.

Then, years later, her brother died in an accident. Sarah's first thought was to *thank God it wasn't one of her children*. She kept recalling this with desperate shame and guilt, as if this meant that she had been responsible for killing her brother. She felt that she *deserved to be punished*.

There was some logic to Sarah's belief, for if these disasters really were her fault, because she had been bad, then being selflessly good might enable her to ward off future disaster.

Sarah looked back at all her past misdeeds as if she could only scrape herself clean enough, all would be well. She tried to be extremely selfless, competent, never angry and always good. Allowing herself pleasure was dangerous, since it might lead to further punishment.

Of course, it also left her feeling exhausted – and resentful of others who seemed to be able to have pleasure in life. And then she needed to punish herself even more.

Deprivation and loss drives hurt and rage; knowledge of hatred drives self-hatred. Then you deserve to be punished. You cannot have sympathy for yourself, and you doubt anyone else's – and if they seem sympathetic, it is only because they have not yet found out how bad you are. For a while you can use frantic manic mechanisms to get away from this state – as Sarah was doing in her efforts to be so good and perfect. But it gets more and more wearing and you can feel more and more alone.

Avoidance of guilt

> *Misfortunes one can endure – they come from outside, they are accidents but to suffer for one's own faults – ah! – there's the sting of life*
>
> (Oscar Wilde, 1893).

Being preoccupied with *huge* faults might, you hope, protect you from noticing smaller but still unwanted ones: smaller, mean ones but, because more specific, very painful.

Sonia's mother had died suddenly, largely as a result of medical negligence, just as Sonia was leaving home. Of course, this was a shocking, desperate loss.

One way in which Sonia responded was to go on an extended, compulsive spending spree. She was hoping to use excitement to manage feelings of outrage at the medical profession – and of deprivation and misery.

This might look like an extreme form of looking after herself, but in fact Sonia barely used all the things she bought, which piled up around her. Attacking herself (and her bank balance) was an attack on the hospital and doctors, displaying how devastatingly they had hurt her, in the indirect, self-destructive way that Freud describes.

But also, by punishing herself in this global way, Sonia hoped to avoid having to worry about her guilt at all the adolescent rows and resentments with her mother, which thinking about caused her so much anguish: which made her fear that she had somehow caused so much damage that her mother had died – and which now she would never have a chance to put right.

Sadness, guilt and grief

Beginning to notice, however fleetingly, that badness, neglect and hostility is not only out there but in oneself is very painful.

When we notice our hostile wishes and deeds, we can feel anxious and guilty at the damage and neglect we have contributed to: damage to those who, however imperfectly, have cared for us, and to ourselves. We can fear the loss of love: our love of ourselves as only good, and the loss of love of others essential to us. These painful, guilty (depressive) worries are different to the extreme paranoid–schizoid, condemnatory depression.

Melanie Klein gave a moving example of facing such mad and bad thoughts, when the death of her adult son in a climbing accident was a stimulus to writing a paper on depression. In the paper, she gives the example of a patient, **Mrs A** – who is, in fact, herself (Klein, 1940).

> Klein describes **Mrs A** gradual recovery from a depressed state: remote, blank and rather suspicious. Her recovery occurred not, as you might imagine, by reassuring herself of her loving feelings for her son, which of course she had, but by facing her uncomfortable *less wanted* feelings which were expressed in a series of dreams.
>
> In one dream *it was not her son who died, but her brother's rival.*
>
> In another, the one who died was *not her son but her loved (and also envied) brother.*
>
> In a final dream*, she was flying in the air with her son. He fell and she had to decide whether to fall too – or whether to stay flying (and live). She chose to live.*

It was desperately sad for Mrs A that her son had died. But what interfered with her mourning and made her feel so suspicious of the world was how she was aware of other envious and destructive feelings in herself: she wanted *someone else's son* to die, not hers; for *her mother's son* to die, not hers. And even though her son had died, *she still wanted to go on and live* – and she was, in a way, punishing him for the hurt he caused her by his death.

Acknowledging the fact of these hateful, attacking feelings towards those whom she also loved, and however understandable, was *agonising* for Mrs A. You might expect that doing so, at a time when she already felt so fragile, she would end up feeling worse. In fact, having faced and grieved for her more hateful feelings, Mrs A felt relieved and hopeful that she now had a mother internally (for her mother was now dead) who would sympathize with her grieving daughter.

Becoming more aware of her hostile feelings made her more firmly in touch with the good, loving ones. Mrs A still needed more time to mourn and face the reality of her loss, but she was no longer in this shut down, blank, mistrustful state. Facing her guilt feelings, however painfully, and despite her sad loss, left Mrs A freer to engage in life and its pleasures once more.

For us too, like Mrs A, noticing what we get up to, how we can be shabby, spoiling and ungrateful, can stir up painful feelings of guilt at damage to those we also love. At the same time it can usher in other feelings: of noticing how we do need others and what they offer in the way of their love and care. Then we are likely to experience feelings of love and gratitude, a wish to make better contact and to make amends.

At those moments we begin to feel more good and sane.

Chapter 10

The good and the sane

It is when the world within us is destroyed, when it is dead and loveless, when our loved ones are in fragments, and we ourselves in helpless despair – it is then we must recreate our world anew, reassemble the pieces, infuse life into dead fragments, recreate life

(Segal, 1952).

If the mad is about what happens when we get rid of unwanted feelings and are left empty, or are filled with hate and blame to protect us from guilt, being sane is about noticing and bearing what is so: who we are in our complicated human selves.

Noticing shameful feelings with a stern regard for truth but without moralism, even with some fondness[1] can bring immense relief. If so, our world is less split into extremes of all bad and all good. There is a possibility of flexibility rather than absolute conviction: where loving feelings can be experienced more fully and mitigate (though not permanently demolish) hateful and envious ones.

> Coming up to an analytic break, **Sam**'s analyst linked a part of a dream he had brought, to his hatred of her at this moment, when she was going away and leaving him.
>
> All of a sudden, vividly, shockingly, Sam felt fury at her: so calm, so smugly pointing out such primitive, childish feelings – and which, worst of all, he felt were true: it made him want to *smash the glass* in her neat, framed pictures. And which he told her.
>
> After a pause, his analyst spoke of how Sam wanted her, in the break, to be here in the room clearing up the mess and thinking of him rather than being away elsewhere, with anyone else. After a long while, Sam commented sadly how he wished his mother could have noticed when he was being *a little sod* – but that this did not mean he was a *monster*.

In an analysis these first moments of *getting it* – that being an infuriating little sod might not be the same as being an unforgivable monster – feels like a revelation. The moment we finally let go of our frantic demand to be seen as perfect, to have it all, the world sighs and calms down. In recognizing our capacity to get up to all kinds of dubious things and to kid ourselves that we aren't *really* doing so, we have more conscious control.

Still, it is not easy. It is painful to stay noticing how messing and spoiling we can be. Though understandable, not a monster, the impact of our actions does damage. We may hope to make amends but still there are opportunities spoiled and relationships lost. The world is greyer. We are all too human. There may be fewer enemies out there, and more within us.

Letting go of this demand to have everything, to be everything doesn't disappear, it just becomes known about. However much we scrabble to be the best there will always be others painfully, enviably better. We can do things, be proud of them, but know them not to be perfect. Sometimes, then, we can bring our conscious, more logical mind to bear, to set limits on, and to reassure, ourselves. Failure, inevitable though it is and always painful, just might not be a disaster. The bar on the high jump is suddenly lowered: it is no longer only about frantic *showing* and *winning*.

If no longer squeaky clean, we will be less condemning of others who no longer carry all the badness: it is easier to empathize. When we have faced some of our darker corners, there is less risk that someone will notice awful hidden things and reject us: it is easier to let others close.

Accepting separateness

In the womb we really are merged, we are *the whole world*, we do have it all.

It is only after birth that we reluctantly discover that wishing for a feed does not fill our belly. There is the unwelcome discovery that our mother and others are separate from us, not merely loyal retainers, humbly looking after us and knowing their place (which, as we might wish it, should be to not have too much of a life enviably separate from us – and yet, at the same time, not too little of a life that their needs and wishes intrude on us).

We may begin to see the world not only from our one-sided view, but through others' eyes, too. The story then becomes more complex: not just one of a mother or father (and, later, friends, partners, children and colleagues) who are neglectful, intrusive or fatally flawed. Their having their own relationships and pleasures in which we are not the centre is never easy.

If others are really separate, with their own lives, the focus pulls back, revealing a picture of parents and others who had, and have, their own difficulties: their own depression, mourning, their own deprivations or abuse from the past which they have had to manage as best they could. Sometimes they have not done this as well as they might.

A parent's difficulties impact on everyone and this is very sad, but can still leave room for mourning and for some better memories to be retrieved. You find that you are not the monster you might have feared – but the parent you complain of may also start to look less of one. Yes, you might wish they could have been different for you, their baby, their child growing up, but it is easy to assume that if only they had got everything right, sacrificed everything for you, you would have been so much better: perfectly loved and, maybe, perfectly loving.

If you were to stand in your parents' shoes, parenting in the circumstances they faced, you might begin to wonder whether you would have done so much better. They failed in the ways they did for all kinds of reasons, good and bad, but rarely because they did not care. And a parent who really does not care almost certainly has their own sad story of deprivation and despair, which they will have managed in those similar self-protective, but maladaptive, ways. In which case it is not so much about forgiving parents but understanding them, separate as they are; of letting go of grievance, and mourning what was not available.

We cannot change the past, but better memories often emerge as a result of the analytic work.

So Sam, in the example above, began to wonder more about his relationship with his difficult mother – and with his father, who did not intervene as much as Sam wished he might have.

He could see how his mother would become infuriatingly controlling when she became anxious. He pointed this out to her, not in the same old one-up way but because he wanted to find a way through to her. Something in his changed attitude made it possible for her to relax more, too.

With his partner, he could notice his terror about being too close, too dependent – and for the first time he became tender, able to see the world through her eyes, not just his own.

Sam had begun to forgive the past for not being as perfect as he would have wished. In doing so he found himself more able to care for others, not just demanding of care from them.

As an analysis moves on, dreams can often be remembered and used more freely. Conflicts can be painfully noticed. Early in his analysis **Frank** had brought a dream:

There was a conical shaped instrument, with strips of brass spiralling round and held in shape by rivets. He liked the craftsmanship and the polished brass: it reminded him of his mother's old Singer treadle sewing machine. He did not know what to make of the dream.

His analyst felt rather shut out by Frank and his absorption with his dream, his hands describing this conical shape: it made her think of a breast, but one with no way in. And this she said.

Frank felt mocking: *analysts always talk about breasts!* But even so it made some sort of weird sense – for it was true that he never had quite found a *way in* to his depressed mother.

Later on in his analysis, another association came to mind about that early dream: to *a street vendor's machine in the Caribbean which held and turned an orange, peeling off the tough outer skin so that it could be squeezed and sucked.*

Frank had an image of how a baby feeding can hold and squeeze his mother's breast. What became clearer was how the problem might not only be with Frank's rather remote mother, but that he, too, needed to be able to squeeze hungrily at life and his relationships.

Approaching the end of his analysis Frank had another dream. In it there was *a dog or a she-wolf. Someone was going to cut off her nipples, a bit like cutting out warts.*

'The dog had two nipples. I was a bit anxious, I thought it would hurt her. I wondered whether an anaesthetic would help, at least she wouldn't be hurt and run off before the second nipple was cut. But then the she-wolf would be left with two cut stubs'.

On waking, Frank was alarmed about this evidence of his biting and cutting feelings: he thought they must be towards the bitch/analyst who, in allowing him to leave, felt abandoning (even if also, he would have felt misunderstood had she argued that he stay longer).

Frank's dream conveyed his wish to cut off the connection between himself and his analyst (who had good things that he could not just *cut off* and take with him) and leave the pain in her.

Having a representation of this idea and a willingness to think about it helped him. He knew he needed to be able to bear the wound: the sadness, anger and loss that he felt at the ending of his analysis, rather than anaesthetize it, if he were to be able to keep the necessary emotional openness (the nipple) to hold on to memories of that helpful experience, and to be able to connect pleasurably with anyone else.

The analyst Wilfred Bion, looking back on his analysis with Melanie Klein, wrote about his movement back and forth between suspicion, developing curiosity and his own perception of his world in the following way:

> *When I was given an interpretation I used to very occasionally feel it was correct; more usually I thought it was nonsense but hardly worth arguing about ... the interpretations that I ignored or did not understand or made no response to, later seemed to have been correct ...*

(Bion, 1991, p. 68).

The patient's smug dismissal of his analyst, 'nonsense', was part of his prickly defensive structure. Part of the slow change was tolerating some curiosity about what his analyst, enviably, was picking up:

She tried to pass on to me her interpretations of the material of which her senses made her aware. But to become efficacious her methods were dependent on my receptivity...

(Bion, 1991, p. 68).

This was different from submitting to his analyst's view as always right in some placatory (or hidden sneering) way. As a result of what his analyst alerted him to, he became more attuned to his own sensed experience, which he learned to trust. Having come to value his analyst's help, being less denigrating of her, he could be separate from her and disagree:

as time passed I became more reconciled to the fact that not even she could be a substitute for my own senses, interpretations of what my senses told me, and a choice between contradictories

(Bion, 1991, p. 68).

Being able to notice, to think, makes us more alive to ourselves and makes conscious choices possible. Recognising that loved ones are separate, not only controlled by us, means that we don't just deserve love and sympathy as of right. If they are separate, then their concern and care is a gift. Noticing ways in which they help, we may feel grateful and more loving: this does not abolish envy but it softens it. This is not always comfortable, not least since the loss of that person and their love would matter, painfully. And that leaves us vulnerable.

Acknowledging such conflicting, shameful impulses involves a mourning process: the loss of our dream of being perfectly right and entitled. It means allowing others to have what is of value – and managing feelings of envy, which do not entirely go but may be lived with. Then, we may find we have less need to deprive ourselves or to attempt frantically to make ourselves feel better, out of feelings of guilt that cannot be consciously acknowledged.

Having faced our flaws to some degree (that source of anxiety, dread and guilt) rather than stuffing them out of mind, then we can begin to knit together the loose ends of what has unravelled. Then (as in the quote at the beginning of this chapter) it becomes more possible to *recreate our world anew, reassemble the pieces, infuse life into dead fragments, recreate life.*

Note

1 As U. A. Fanthorpe put it, p. 43.

Part III

Conflict through the life stages

Without contraries is no progression. Attraction and repulsion, reason and energy, love and hate, are necessary to human existence
(Blake, 1966[1790], *The Marriage of Heaven and Hell*).

Returning to the account of the developing child, conflicts that originate in infancy and early childhood reverberate through later life.

The next challenge to be faced is Freud's Oedipus complex. This is a story of love and hatred, of exclusion and of threat, of the sense we make of our gendered body, sexual feelings and the relationships we make. Freud's ideas can be disturbing, provoking – but even so, provide fascinating food for thought.

Chapter 11

The young child and Oedipus

When the king of Thebes heard a prophecy that his new-born son, Oedipus, would one day kill him and would marry the boy's mother, he sent his baby son off to be killed. The baby, left to die of exposure, was found and adopted by the king of the neighbouring state.

As a young man, Oedipus was horrified to hear of the prophecy, and to forestall it he left his country and his presumed parents. On his journey, he encountered an irascible elderly man, got into a fight with, and killed, him. It turned out that the stranger was the king of Thebes. Oedipus travelled there, married the new widow and became king.

Many years and three children later, when all kinds of disasters were affecting the kingdom, Oedipus sought for the reason: he was told that he had indeed killed his father and married his mother. He gouged out his eyes in despair
(Greek myth).

In Freud's Oedipus complex, as well as his passionate infantile dependence on, and love for, his mother, his wish to be her only baby, the young boy (and girl) also wants to be the one to *give her babies* and to get rid of his father. At the same time, he wants to have his father all to himself, to be loved by him, and to get rid of his mother. When his parents are together, he is excluded and enraged. This is a source of unwinnable conflict.

It was an extraordinary opportunity for Freud to test out his ideas when a colleague brought his concerns about his 5-year-old son, who had developed phobias about going out. Freud saw the little boy only once, and worked by advising the boy's father on how he might speak to his son.

Little Hans (Freud, 1909b)[1]

Five-year-old Little Hans had developed a sudden fear of horses after seeing one being beaten in the street: he was horrified – but also fascinated. The boy had been extremely close to his mother and he longed for a return to a previous summer with her, when his father had visited for weekends only and before his baby sister (now 18 months old) had been born.

Little Hans seems to have been a delightful, curious little boy, pleased and relieved to talk with his father (under Freud's direction) about his fears, his dreams and his less acceptable feelings, without his father being shocked or judgemental.

Little Hans was very interested in his 'widdler'. He was fascinated by the large size of horses' widdlers, and thought his mother probably had *a huge one* too. He enjoyed his penis being touched in washing and touching himself – and he seemed unconcerned when his mother threatened that if he kept touching his widdler it would be '*cut off*'. He saw his baby sister naked and commented on her '*sweet little widdler*'.

Little Hans was interested in the idea of having babies himself and associated them with his *lumf* – his faeces. He thought that he too, like his mother, might receive babies from his father. He also wanted to marry his mother, and thought that if his father married *his* mother, then all would be well.

Under Freud's guidance, the boy's father spoke to him of his hostile wishes, suggesting that he might wish that the father would fall down or be whipped, like the horse in the street, so that Little Hans could get his mother all to himself. The boy greeted this idea with relief.

He told his father of anxious thoughts that a plumber came:

and first he took away my behind with a pair of pincers, and then gave me another, and then the same with my widdler (p. 95).

He worried that if he fell in the bath, his mother might not rescue him. Again he agreed with his father's suggestion that he feared that his mother would no longer love him if she knew of his hostile wishes: wishes such as that his baby sister would drown.

The boy's fears receded.

Little Hans's drives and impulses are bodily. He gains pleasure from the sensual excitement in different parts of his body, including his genitals. He has happy thoughts of having babies, like his mother; receiving them, like her, from his father. He also wants to use his penis in a lively, potent and possessive way.

Little Hans loves his mother, but he is also a rival with her for his father's love. He is in deadly rivalry with his father for the exclusive love of his mother – but he also loves him. He attempts to solve this unwinnable dilemma by pushing away his hostile feelings but, as a result, the outside world feels dangerous: horses might bite him, the plumber will take away his *behind* and his *widdler*, and his mother will no longer want to rescue him if he slips in the bath.

The fact that his father can talk to Little Hans, non-moralistically of his hostile impulses, as well as his loving ones, helps to free him from his anxieties in a way which reassurance had not been able to do. Little Hans's father does not collapse in the face of his son's passionate conflicting feelings (like the horse in the street), nor does he furiously (bitingly) retaliate.

What me! Marry my mother! (or my father!)

As an adolescent or an adult it is easy to look at a middle-aged mother and wonder how this could ever have been so. If Freud is right, our quick dismissal could also carry a past anxious threat: *you cannot have her: you must give her up or you will be punished.*

But look at a baby (such as you once were) in his mother's arms, or a toddler rushing back to her for comfort or diving between them when she is in an embrace with his father. That's the sort of passion of which Freud speaks.

Unconscious wishes

Unconscious wishful thinking is about *playing* with ideas, different and contradictory ones at the same time – and this is not the same as a concrete, conscious wish.

> One delighted, excited 4-year-old was bouncing on his parents' bed one Sunday morning and told his mother, '*I am going to put my willy in you and fill you up like at the petrol station!*'
>
> He might not have had any conscious thought about how or where he would put his willy, but he felt his bodily excitement and had the happy belief that he had good things to offer and that his mother would be pleased to receive them from him.

A child who is excited at the idea of having the mother or father all to him (or her-) self in every way – sensually, genitally, *filling his mother up like at the petrol station* – is not the same as concretely wanting sexual contact, in the way an adult would understand it. Had the little boy been asked quite how he would do this, he would have felt embarrassed and angry that his happy game was being intruded upon and spoiled.

> Two young sisters of 7 and 9 brought their Barbies in bridal dresses to their father, wanting to know *which one he'd like to marry*?

Their hugs with their father are likely to be associated with good feelings in their bodies, including in their genitals; they might wish to replace their mother and do with their father whatever exciting thing their parents do in bed together; they might wish to have his baby, but it is not literal sexual intercourse that they want. They want to *win* their father, to be his princess, his one-and-only. What is so painfully conveyed is that they cannot win him exclusively, not only over each other, but over their mother, too.

When physical boundaries are crossed in sexual abuse, it is confusing and disturbing for the child. There may be something tempting and exciting, for the offer apparently is of being *especially loved* and having a *special secret*;

being in league with one parent and leaving the other out: apparently winning the Oedipal drama. For a child who is otherwise deprived, this can be particularly inviting.

But in fact the offer is not about special love and concern for the child. Rather, it is a cover for the interests of the adult who wants to use the child in a particular way and is too self-absorbed to notice the child's distress – or who is pleased to have confusion felt by someone other than him (or her)-self. The child can then feel cheated and exploited, but also guiltily complicit in the exclusion of the other parent.

Similarly, when the child wishes to get his father (or another rival) out of the way, when his (or her) ideas about death are so immature, he would not only be pleased were damage really to occur. Indeed, when a death happens, it is very worrying for the child: not only does he lose his parents to their sad loss, but in addition he believes that it is somehow his doing.

> One **anxious 5-year-old little girl** was taken to see Winnicott (1971). The little girl, whose younger brother had a congenital heart problem, could not play.
>
> In the consulting room, while he spoke to her mother, the little girl put her soft toy lamb in Winnicott's pocket. He suggested to her that her little lamb *might like a friend to play with* from the toy box in the corner. She took a donkey and laid him *in bed, side by side* with her lamb, as if to keep them safe from anything more dangerously lively. He suggested to her that the two animals *might have dreams*. This seemed to help her play more freely.

Winnicott was conveying to the little girl and to her mother that when something bad happens – like a baby born with a heart defect – it is not a result of any lively ideas or phantasies, however murderous; that it is indeed safe, important even, to be able to play – not only *nicely*, but boisterously, too.

We may hate reality and want to challenge it and the parent who tells us 'no'. At the same time, there is a vital security when parents are able to keep limits on our behalf. As a child we need our parents (and others) to be able to protect our imaginative space so that we can play with all kinds of phantasies and wishes: greedy, possessive and loving, as well as attacking ones, and it is a relief (if also a disappointment) to realize that there is a limit to our excited imagined powers.

Sexual difference

There are other discoveries to make, too.

> When out of nappies, as well as in the bath, you are suddenly able to see and touch what previously you had not: your genitals, that fascinating, sensitive body part. What do you discover *down there*? How does it

compare to what you see of your parents dressing? Or of an older sibling, a playmate, or a baby when it is changed?

A troubling fact is that not everyone has the same: some have a penis and others not. This is a fundamental early part of categorizing the world and bewildering if this sorting is undermined:

> Two and a half-year-old **Sam** was beside himself when his mother described the young child next door as a 'girl'. He knew perfectly well she was a boy: he'd seen her out of nappies and seen what protruded from her belly! (His mother had to explain to him that it wasn't a penis he had seen, but her belly button that was still sticking out.)

It is fascinating and important. No wonder young children go off in small huddles to scrutinize who has what.

Threat

Freud argues that for the young child who has loving and murderous feelings towards both parents, the recognition of sexual difference creates an anxious threat.

For the little boy, if not everyone has a penis, his could not be taken from him – *could it*? He risks not only the loss of love for his possessive and jealous wishes, but also the loss of his so-valued penis. Then a part of his pleasure in holding his penis may be sheer relief: *Yes! Here it is, alive and present – for now at least!*

And, Freud argues, for the little girl is the dreadful thought: why *doesn't she have one? What has happened to hers?* (I speak of her more, shortly.)

But 'castration': really!

When Little Hans's mother first threatened, however playfully, to cut off his widdler if he kept playing with it, the 5-year-old did not seem to take her seriously: only later did he suddenly feel threatened and become incapacitated with anxiety. Freud argued that the mother's threat was given a dreadful credibility by the sight of his little sister having no penis.

Nowadays, when children are more likely to see their parents naked, are given sexual information earlier, and when parents may be less likely, however playfully, to threaten to cut off their genitals, the idea of fearing castration might seem ridiculous.

It is only at the level of nightmares, of earliest dreads, that there remains a ghastly plausibility of a threat to what is most precious and intimate. In torture, a threat to the genitals is the worst, and homo- or heterosexual rape a way of humiliating an enemy. The dreaded assault is depicted fictionally when

James Bond's genitals are smashed in the film, *Casino Royale*, and all too literally in the real world, as in the attacks on prisoners in Abu Ghraib (during the Second Iraq War) and elsewhere.

Humiliation

The little boy might want to believe that his penis signifies possession and power – but still he faces loss and disappointment.

Little Hans wants to be not only as big as his father, he wants to be *bigger, better* than him, *now.* He may be pleased to think he will be like his father in the future, the one who can partner someone like his mother and give her babies. But for now he is small: he has to wait. It is his father who can offer something particular to his mother – and not he. And that is a sore blow.

For boys and men there is an ever-present risk of being symbolically castrated: shown up as *small* and *unmanly* in comparison with other men, or in the feared mocking eyes of women. To avert such risk of shame and dishonour, *bigging it* over a rival or a loved figure can seem the only way to restore self-worth.

A significant proportion of men who end up in prison can't read. When finally helped to learn to read, in a class with other adults also struggling, their sense of amazed pride and pleasure, quite the opposite of *cool*, was very moving. (Ryan, 2015)

This can happen at a group level too. So the state reaction to the attack on the Twin Towers of 9/11 (such a symbol of hyper-masculinity) arguably used extreme force to counter feelings of humiliation and that impulse overrode any more thoughtful ability to notice who the perpetrators really were.[2]

Little Hans also wants to be like his mother, so loved and vital to him as she is. He wants to have babies in his tummy and produce them like his *lumf*, as she does. He wants to be maternal, to be loved by his father as she is, and to care for a baby as he is still cared for by her. And he cannot in that way. He may manage by turning away with extra enthusiasm towards his father, claiming that boys and men have *everything* and his mother and girls *nothing*.

When femininity, and what the mother represents, is repudiated out of anxious threat, then pleasure in receiving nurture in an open way can be lost, as well as pleasure in caring for another. If feelings of dependence mean being emasculated, the boy can hate women who stir up such feelings of longing – and this can interfere with his capacity to love, and feel loved, in turn. In this way he can be left emotionally lacking.

Oedipus and the girl

So what does the young girl make of discovering that some have this interesting possession, a penis – but not her, or other girls? Might she wonder *why not*? *Has hers been taken from her*? Is she deprived? Does she feel herself to be (as Freud put it) *castrated*?

It is true, of course, that in the era in which Freud wrote, the lack of a penis represented not only the lack of a fascinating body part. In a world where women had less direct outlet for their energy, excitement or power other than wait to be chosen by, or pleasing, a man, nursing sick relatives, or finding self-worth indirectly through the achievements of children, then not having a penis signified being cut off from activity, independence and potency: being socially and politically castrated.

Freud's point was not that girls *are* castrated, less valuable: he was saying that emotionally they have to grapple with the fact of their not having this exciting body part. And if in every other area toddlers and young children want to take what is so interesting that another has, why would that little girl not feel, to some degree, perturbed and envious? (Later analysts have suggested that particularly strong feelings of penis envy are more likely related to deprivation in the girl's early relation to her mother (Klein, 1975).)

The little girl can manage this by pushing it from her conscious mind. She will have some awareness of her own pleasurable genital sensations (Horney, 1935; Klein, 1975), but if it is too disturbing to discover that whatever else she has, it is *not a penis*, she may be inhibited in discovering her interior genitals.[3]

Freud argues that the girl holds her mother responsible for depriving her of the interesting penis, as she herself is deprived. This then can be a source of unease and resentment. The young girl turns away from her mother and turns to her father and all that he offers: but she faces a problem. She can hope to be like her father in his masculine activity but she still has to struggle with the meaning of a *something* interesting which she has not got: she is not like him in this bodily way, and takes this into account in her sense of her worth and who she is.

The little girl can defiantly decide she does not care a bit: it doesn't matter anyway, but that quality of defiance may suggest that there is something disturbing to be kept out of mind. She may be consoled by an idea of possessing something very special in the future, such as a baby, but these possibilities do not offer the current reassurance and pleasure that the boy's little penis does to him.

She may hope to supplant her mother, be her father's special loved one and gain power by being the *object of desire*, but in a passive way, wanting to be loved and desired rather than to be actively desiring.

Girls and women have the psychological task of finding a self-worth that is not to do with defiant denial – being 'laddish', 'ballsy' – or with masochistic submission to men. A girl may want to be encouraged to venture bravely out into the world in her own right, not only to nurture those who do. She needs to find a way to feel potent and active without devaluing her female body and abilities. If she constantly has to prove herself to be as good as or better than men, this can get in the way of her pleasure at what she *does* have.

At some moments, Freud wrote as if he assumed 'femininity' and 'passivity' were one and the same. But Freud did not think that girls and women have, or should have, only passive, receptive, 'feminine' drives (or boys and men, only active ones). So, with 18-year-old Dora,[4] Freud was not saying that she *should be passive*: he was saying that she did have her own clear, active, sexual wishes and ideas and that it was her denial of these that led to her symptoms. If Dora could acknowledge her conflicting feelings, then she could take decisions based on what she felt, rather than covering them over.

In that sense *feminine* and *masculine* elements are an important part in the make-up of both: boy and girl, man and woman. Freud was challenging but also liberating to women.

Women's ambitions and successes in many fields have moved on since Freud was writing, and biology clearly is not only destiny. Even so, girls and young women can still feel that their self-worth is dependent on their being seen as desirable by others. Even now, they are more likely to starve themselves, cut themselves and suffer low self-esteem. They speak out less than boys and young men, and still, it seems, successful women can be reluctant to ask for higher pay.

Is it possible that there is more than prejudice and expectation alone that leave girls and women anxious about making claims? Could Freud be right that there is a disappointment that is so disturbing that girls and women make it unconscious? And if that were so, then it would be helpful to notice and mourn that loss consciously, rather than it have an impact out of conscious sight.

The Oedipal blow is one of the facts of life. The Oedipus myth speaks to the pain of when a relationship between two people has to widen to include another. The pain of being, even for some of the time, the one on the outside: the feelings of hatred most of us will recognize – and the fear that our hatred makes us unlovable.

Notes

1 And see Appendix C.
2 In that, whatever his other deeds, Saddam Hussein did not sponsor al-Qaida.
3 French analysts such as MacDougall (1995) and Chasseguet-Smirgel (1970) have added to this account, as have some British ones such as Mitchell, J. (1974), Laufer (1988), Breen (1993), Birksted-Breen (1996) and Raphael-Leff and Perelberg (1997).
4 Described on p. 24.

Chapter 12

The child
Resolving or evading Oedipus

This next stage, roughly between the ages of 5 and 11, may seem to be a quieter time. Freud saw it as a giving up of the Oedipal struggle and a turning away to less threatening and intellectual challenges in latency.

Biological development as well as Oedipal disappointment provide a spur for the young child to look out into the world beyond the family with its challenges, threats and all that it might have to offer.

> Your world becomes bigger – and you smaller in relation to it. You may have to manage the arrival of a new baby in the family – or the attacks of elder siblings. You begin school and learn to manage without the presence of parents. You have to learn to wait, and to share; to ride a bike with a combination of physical skill and courage; to tie shoelaces, sound out letters, do sums. All the resources you have been able to learn up until this time help manage disappointment – or have not yet developed.
>
> The degree to which you feel known and accepted, with your loving feelings as well as hostile ones, makes it possible to have some sense of buoyancy as you move out into the wider world. It affects the resilience with which you manage the challenges and limitations of school; your capacity to connect with other children and with adults, when you are not always the best, and tolerate the stresses of learning with some enthusiasm.
>
> *Can you reassure yourself and not despair when others do better?*
> *Can you reach out for comfort and friendship from others or do you turn away?*
> *Do you resort to bullying as a way of getting uncertain, vulnerable feelings out there safely into someone else who you can despise and mock?*

The pain of the Oedipal blow can be mitigated if the little boy (or girl) feels that not everything has been lost: he may not be his mother's one and only but he still has a special, if not perfect, place in her mind.

> When you can say 'no' and are not seen as just disobedient; when you are anxious and are not seen as stupid but given support to manage; when

feeling hurt does not mean being weak; or excited and hopeful does not mean showing off, then you are freer to find a sense of yourself. With luck, you have a father, or others, available to help you manage this transition and help you discover the pleasures of the outside world.

But, for the young child who has had less experience of his feelings being acknowledged, less sense of being firmly held in his mother's and his father's mind, this task is more difficult. The more resentful he feels, so he may fear that his place has been irrevocably spoiled by his hidden attack. When his emotional base feels less firm, the child can cling and feel unable to freely leave.

Parents' difficulties

A mother and a father can have their own Oedipal difficulties with allowing in a third person.

A mother who finds the bond with her baby very gratifying can find it hard to allow a partner in to share and can push him away. When she has unmet emotional needs, she can want to hold her child close: he, who is her special one. A father who has difficulties tolerating the mother's bond with her baby can withdraw or he can become hostile, rather than help to pull her back towards their adult partnership. The couple then is not the parental one, but the mother and child.

This can be seductive for the child: he has *won* the Oedipal battle, he has his mother – but it can also be engulfing. Without the father's support for the mother and the child, it is harder for the child to feel free to become more separate. To feel love or desire towards someone else can seem a betrayal of her.

Parents can be unavailable for many reasons: a mother or a father may be depressed or stressed, alcoholic, abusive, or just absent. External pressures may be extreme. Family break-up is one great stressor. Then the child loses out on that firm support, as in the following case.

> **Brian** was 6 when his parents were breaking up. It was not just a one-off event: it changed the course of all their lives.
>
> His mother was in a frenzy and new partners came and went. After a number of years, she finally settled down with a new partner and had another baby – though life was still stormy. His father was attentive, but miserable and remote. Brian felt there was just no room for him and he retreated miserably and furiously in an entrenched state.
>
> Many years later, Brian came into an analysis. There, for a very long time, he was silent, feeling that he had to keep simmering hatreds and resentments under a tight lid. He felt like bursting! Only slowly could he express any of these feelings in words, and find that disaster did not ensue.

When the parents have a bond, however stressed, that still contains admiration or love, the parents' sexual partnership can be envied and desired. When a father is abandoning or attacking and is denigrated, then it has an impact on the child's love relationships and sexual desires.

To the degree that compliance is based on threat and fear of punishment, then feelings of resentment and defiance are a powerful part of the mix. A child who cannot challenge a parent because of a worry that they are vulnerable or quick to anger, learns to keep quiet and manage alone. He may resent them, but to challenge them might cause any sort of stability to collapse. If the little boy (or girl) just submits to his father, then he cannot find the enthusiasm and buoyancy to move on into the outside world. Equally, if he triumphs over his father, defiantly or in a hidden way, devaluing him, then he loses out on a robust father *internally* to support him.

There is our experience of parents: their real strengths and difficulties. But it is not only that.

The parents that we feel ourselves to have (our parents internally), are also affected by us: by *our* wishes, envy and resentments. Little Hans's father and mother seemed to have been loving and playful with their son[1]: it was his unacknowledged wishes towards them that made his world seem quite so fearful.

Parents internally

Freud assumed that all being well we do, mostly, resolve our Oedipal conflict. We may not be 'His Majesty the Baby' (Freud 1914b), but if we can tolerate that loss without too much grievance and resentment, if we can acknowledge what parents have which is valuable and enviable, then we can identify with each of them in particular ways. (This, rather than *being* them, or *taking over* from them.)

But we don't always manage that. There are ways we can short-circuit Oedipal reality, by depleting parents' goods, individually and together as a couple, having anything that might be special, supportive and pleasurable. But if so, we too are depleted – in part by our undermining of them.

The little boy can claim that his little penis is all that his mother needs and wants – but if he can notice, woundingly, what his father offers her, then he has a sense of parents who are of value to each other, and to him. He has firmer figures internally. In time, he can have his own sexual relationship and, like his parents, he will have good and loving things to offer a partner.

If the little girl just dismisses her mother and identifies with a very hard, exciting penis/father, then she can present herself as tough, endlessly compe-tent – but can feel that a more vulnerable part of her has been lost. A little girl who can bear to notice that her father loves and admires her mother, however imperfectly, is supported: she can feel that as well as what she has that is like her father, as a woman she has worth, too. If not, her sense of herself as lovable is impaired.

In **Louise**'s accounts of her parents' relationship they were absent from each other, each of them in separate rooms.

When her analyst spoke of these distant parents, Louise was surprised: she brought forward many other memories of when they were happily together. She thought they had been in love.

Only then was there some more room to think about her relationship with her husband, which was loving but rather non-sexual. Louise could not feel herself to be desirable.

It was as if, by pushing out of mind and thereby depriving her parents of their loving, sexual relationship, she could not have one either.

It is not easy tolerating our admiration and envy of others, but if we cannot, then we can't learn from or emulate them:

Felix saw how his quiet, rather shy father could relax and enjoy playing the guitar with a couple of other friends. At 11, he wanted that, too. He asked his father to teach him but was furious when his father did so – and when he suggested that Felix might find it easier to learn from another teacher. He did not practise much.

Felix wanted to be as good as (and preferably better than) his father straight away. He did not want to have to practise, fail again and again, and still feel it worth doing. He raged at reality (*too hard*); at himself (*too stupid*); and at his father (who if he was *any good* would have made it effortlessly easy). Hatred was easier, made him feel stronger than facing the humiliation that his father had something special that he could not achieve without effort.

Felix may, or may not, decide that learning the guitar is for him. But it will be a great help to him if he can learn to manage the pull into hatred, blame and giving up, and bear to let his father help him in that.

Who would not have wry sympathy with Felix? The trouble is that if he, or we, cannot find a way through, then we remain limited.

There can be real difficulties to manage, but we can also use these for our own ends, as the following example shows.

Gerry's mother was mourning the loss of her sister after a lengthy illness, and was often tearful and remote.

When Gerry wailed at leaving his mother to go to school, she would weep, too: then he would feel that he and she were united in grief at their separation. In addition, Gerry hoped, it won his mother's attention away from the new baby in the family, and from his father.

In one way this attention was exciting and gratifying, but it was also trapping. When, at school, there were moments when he began to forget his mother and enjoy himself, he felt that he was betraying her and he might lose his special place with her – just as he hated her when she turned away from him.

If his father had been more able to reclaim his mother, then together his parents might have encouraged Gerry out into the world, with less fear that he had caused irreparable damage to his mother: it might feel safer, less trapping, to return to his mother for comfort. But when his father was close to his mother, Gerry found this intolerable and he raged.

The belief that he was his mother's rescuer meant that Gerry never quite had to give up his Oedipal dream – but it was increasingly burdensome as he grew up. Since he had not learned to have less than everything, as an adult he found it impossible to have a satisfying love relationship. As soon as he began to feel loving and settled, he would dread becoming trapped (as with his mother): then he would use feelings of hatred to pull himself away.

Years later he was able to explore this intense, conflictual situation in the transference relationship with his analyst, without her collapsing or retaliating: where she could sympathize with him, but stand her ground.

Siblings

It is often the arrival of a new baby that can stir up feelings of exclusion. Hatred that might otherwise be directed at parents can instead be directed at the newcomer.

For some, slowly, grudgingly, a brother or sister can come to be seen as having their uses – as playmate, as fall-guy, as an ally in standing up to parents. When a relationship with a sibling is hostile, it can seem so much better to have been an only child and have all a parent's attention – but it can also be a relief when not: when a sibling's presence can allow more room to get on without a parent's too intrusive eye. When there is a sense of sufficient parental resources, then siblings can sometimes be protective and helpful, too.

An example of some of the growing anxieties that could not be managed is that of **Richard**, a 10-year-old boy seen daily by Melanie Klein over four months (Klein, 1945; 1961).[2]

Richard was inhibited, fearful of other children and unable to attend school. He clung to his mother in a childish way – seeing himself as *her chick*. The thought of moving towards adolescence and genital sexuality filled him with horror and dismay.

Six weeks into the work, Klein was away in London for two weeks. During this time Richard asked his mother, as he had asked her a number of times before, whether it would hurt him to deliver babies. His mother explained again the man's part in intercourse and he replied with disgust and anxiety that he *would not like to do that with his genital.*

What is unusual is not the question or the anxiety, but that the level of horror was such that Richard could only circle round it and could not find any sense of hope or resilience to help him.

Klein put the fears expressed in Richard's play and drawings into words, clearly and warmly, such that the boy could begin to think about them. She spoke not only of Richard's loving feelings towards his parents but his sexual and his hostile ones, too – and of such feelings to her, his analyst, in the consulting room.

In the first session after her return she described how

> Richard was anxious and listless: he barely looked at his analyst. He described the village they were living in as a 'pigsty'; was anxious about toadstools he found in the garden which might be 'poisonous'; and was dismayed to find in a book a picture of an 'awful monster'
>
> (1961, p. 191).

Klein took up his hostile feelings. She said that now she had become a bad pigsty Mrs K, by her leaving him. This was made worse by his thought that she had been meeting up with her husband, like a Hitler/Daddy – and this made him want to bomb her.

At this Richard's feelings suddenly changed: he showed a flood of relief and love for his analyst, her beauty, her silver hair, the mountainside . . .

Richard's freer mood lasted. The next day in his play he

> *bumped two of his ships together; Rodney (which represented his mother) and Vampire – which he said was himself.*
>
> Touching the ships together had already been understood as representing intercourse – and Klein spoke of his wishes to have intercourse with his mother.[3]
>
> Richard then placed all the ships in an ordered row: his father, mother, elder brother, himself, the family dog . . .
>
> Klein said that what she had spoken of made him anxious and that he now wanted to keep the peace and give up his wishes for his mother . . .
>
> Richard spoke of *being his mummy's chick . . . Chicks do run after their Mums . . .but then chicks have to do without them, because the hens don't look after them anymore and don't care for them.*

In the following session:

> *Richard was anxious again, this time about a boy he felt threatened by in the hotel. He sucked on a pencil.*
>
> Klein said the pencil was like his father's good penis, which he wanted to suck on but also to bite – and then his father felt bad and dangerous. This seemed to help the 10-year-old.

Richard made a lively drawing showing a fish covering a baby fish with a fin, but for the first time he wasn't one of the babies. His father was represented as a small octopus among the rushes. There was a submarine, Sunfish, underneath the ship, Rodney (his mother). In the air there was a plane circling. He did not know where he was in the drawing.

Klein thought Richard was the son/Sunfish

– and he rather cheerfully pointed out how the periscope went into Rodney.

Approaching puberty, Richard wanted to find a way to not only be a baby chick in relation to his mother: he wanted to find a way to feel that he had something good and exciting to offer her.

He wanted to be able to feel he could push up against her, excite her, attack her without having to fear that he had destroyed her. In the work with Klein, he found a way to access more hopeful genital feelings towards his mother. He needed his father's help to do this: his pencil/penis – and his involved support.

Klein interpreted Richard's jealous, active genital desires for his mother, his fears for damage to her and also his wanting to protect, care for and give babies to her. She also described his rivalrous and his loving feelings towards his excluded father. Klein was saying *this is so. This is normal. Even if it is also conflictual and painful.*

Only when Richard could begin to accept that he had aggressive feelings as well as loving ones towards his (previously idealized) mother, his father, brother and his analyst could he begin to feel that there was something more solid in him and in relation to his parents. His parents felt more solid, too.

To the degree that we mock others as a way of protecting our self-esteem, so we can dread the mockery that may be turned back on us. It can make it safer to conform than to not know, disagree, or to be different from others. We cannot feel free to have our own thoughts; to be *ourselves* (whatever that might turn out to be). Enthusiasm and creativity that is evident earlier on can become increasingly constrained.

The artist, Mark Rothko, ran a free-school for youngsters in the Brooklyn of the 1930s which aimed to foster children's creative expression: he described how, by the age of 9, all children turned to a mimicry of what was expected, despite the teachers' best efforts (Rothko, 2006).

If we are unable to re-find that potent creativity, that more playful authentic *us*, then it is limiting in later life. When we have more experience of feeling recognized as our own unsure, developing person, then we have more basis for enthusiasm. We are more able to risk disagreement, disapproval and sometimes just being wrong without it being a disaster. When we can manage feelings of rivalry, envy and jealousy, then we are able to make use of others' help.

This becomes a part of our superego (or a sense of parents internally) which, while representing painful reality, can also feel protective and helpful.

The super-ego

Freud thought that we resolve the Oedipal struggle by internalising a version of our parents. Managing by sullenly submitting or by defiance, we can miss out on what we do need to be able to take from parents: a superego which is not only prohibiting, but can be helpful and protective. Some prohibitions we need to accept as a part of reality: they may feel cruel, but they are not so. We need help to restrain our id impulses: just turning to an open, or a hidden, tantrum is not useful in managing life long term.

Anna Freud pointed out how helpful our superego (and the firm identification with parents and admired figures, community support and religious morality) can be (Freud, A. & Burlingham,1974, pp. 130–131). When firm, but not rigid, it offers us guidelines which can be vital in situations of stress - and when not, we are vulnerable.

> In 1968, a group of young American men just out of basic training were in their first tour of duty in Vietnam. They had to manage the horror and terror of members of their company being shot or blown up by unseen assailants. Most used drugs to help them manage what was otherwise intolerable. Ten weeks in, they killed and mutilated the bodies of five hundred women, children and old people in the village of **My Lai** (Simm, 1989).
>
> Some described wanting revenge after the death of one of their comrades. One described his savagery as a response to the horror he felt at discovering that the figure he had shot, running away and apparently carrying a rifle, was in fact a woman with a baby.

Who can say that any of us would do any better in such horrific circumstances?

> But a small number of the young men were able to resist this pull into savagery (and they shot over the heads of the fleeing villagers). They had some firmer relation internally to parents, community and sometimes to a faith, which helped them. They had a helpful firm superego that protected them from acting on the worst of their terrified and savage impulses.

Managing Oedipal passions and disappointment is not easy – but it has advantages, too. Finding that we cannot be our mother's one and only pulls us away from the early dependent relationship with our mother to the interests of the father and on to the outside world. It allows for relationships with others – for her and for ourselves. Feelings of love and being loved can help mitigate feelings of resentment and hatred.

When the parents whom we identify with are alive in our mind, they are helpful even in their absence. It is a great help to the young child as he (or she) moves out into the wider world with its challenges, stresses and inevitable humiliations. When this sense of internal parents, however imperfectly loved and loving, is less secure, then it is harder, lonelier.

Notes

1 Page 75.
2 And see Appendix F.
3 Klein spoke in a more literal, bodily way than is generally used now – but which Richard seems to have taken in his stride (Spillius, 1994).

Chapter 13

Early adolescence and the changing body

The summer she was fifteen, Melanie discovered she was made of flesh and blood.
O, my America, my new found land. She embarked on a tranced voyage, exploring
the whole of herself, clambering her own mountain ranges, penetrating the moist
richness of her secret valleys, a physiological Cortez, da Gama or Mungo Park
(Carter, 1967).

In early adolescence, our bodies and their changes shunt us on inexorably from
childhood out towards the adult world, and there we face a new, alarming
reality. It may be exciting – but there are unknown terrors too, in this newly
sexual world, much as the explorers above faced in discovering rivers, jungles
and mountains of the New World.

> Your body is more out of control than at any stage since being potty
> trained. No longer does it have its recognizable, familiar, taken-for-granted
> shape. Height shoots up – or it doesn't while everyone else's does; hair
> sprouts in armpits and on genitals; new hormones, new smells, new bodily
> fluids – and newly unformulated desires. The gap between the desirable
> bodies displayed in magazines, honed and retouched, and your strange new
> body in all its gawkiness and uncertainty can seem hopelessly large. It will
> never be *as good as* ... *as big a*s ... how it *should be*!
> Your body and its urges expel you from a prior, unquestioned and
> relatively safe state. You are no longer *little*. It may be exciting but there are
> important losses too - including the loss of physical touch with parents, which
> previously had been such an important reassurance.

A boy's growing penis is a source of intense new stimuli, astonishing excitement – and anxiety. As poet Adrian Mitchell put it:

> *It was like keeping a puppy in your underpants*
> *A secret puppy you weren't allowed to show to anyone ...*

(Mitchell, 1996)

While the boy's penis is visible and accessible, his hidden desires can be troubling.

> When 11-year-old **Harry** was masturbating, his younger sister rumpled in her nightdress came to mind. He was horrified: he was a disgusting pervert. What would anyone think if they knew! And anyway, how could anyone want him to do *that* to them?

The boy's external penis and his impulse to action and penetration can mean that he avoids noticing anything more interior, such as anxieties and needs, which may seem insufficiently masculine.

A girl's breasts swell. She bleeds and might be doubled-up with pain. She leaks in ways she has not since a baby in nappies. A girl can have particular anxieties to do with her more hidden genitals. What does she have *down there, in there*? Is she allowed to touch – or gain any pleasure from doing so? But if she cannot find the answers to some of these questions for herself, how on earth can she allow any pleasure from anyone else's touch?

Suddenly, in early adolescence, she is the object of others' curious, sexual eyes, which may be a source of excitement, but often, too, of intrusion and alarm. Seeing herself in this way can interfere with her discovering more about who she finds herself to be.

It is not only the fact of the body and all its astonishing changes. There is also what it represents. A girl having her first menstruation and her capacity to have a real baby, or a boy with his voice breaking and hair growing on his still-boyish face, know that life will never be that safe or familiar again.

Freud's ideas have played an important part in dissolving the prohibitions and hypocrisy that were so strong over 100 years ago. But have we replaced those constrictions and expectations with other ones?

For, in Freud's day, socially it was expected and accepted that the child moving into early adolescence would be protected from having to manage sexual situations too early, shutting down out of prohibition and anxiety in *latency*. The young adolescent's body might be changing, they might have sexual feelings and fantasies, they might be developing in alarming and disturbing ways – but for the time being they could still turn away to other less threatening activities, including learning. They could take time to adjust to their changing body and its drives, without having to take action too soon.

But now, an early adolescent can feel that there is a premature pressure to be grown-up, sexual and cool, and will then miss out on the protected space allowing for them to move back and forwards between childhood and early adulthood: time to explore sexuality at their own unforced pace.

Early adolescents try out adult sexuality, trying on provocative clothes, make-up and gestures.

Alice, at 12, wanted to dress as the images of models she saw all around, experimenting with a lot of make-up and wearing a tight dress which showed her breasts, which seemed so large and not really hers. Seeing admiration and desire in others' eyes was exciting, if alarming, too, but she didn't feel herself and she was not sure she knew any longer who herself was. She no longer knew how to be comfortable around boys and they, too, were no longer natural around her. Was this what growing up was? Just getting good at putting on the appearance of being cool?

Treating your body as an object in this way can be alienating: no longer your own, but to be viewed through the eyes of another. Handing over that body to be stimulated by someone else can feel exciting but also dangerous, stirring up, as it does, not only adult sexual feelings but dependent, vulnerable ones, too. Not since being a toddler has your body been so intimately attended to.

When this newly sexual body feels just too dangerous, one way of attempting control is in holding back sexual growth in anorexia. Another way is to turn to heavy use of drugs or alcohol, allowing sexual experimentation by blanking out anxieties.

Changing relation with parents

Parents, who previously had been more or less relied on, are suddenly looked at and challenged. Recognizing that parents have flaws and vulnerabilities, and sometimes really do not know, can leave an adolescent feeling excited and superior, but it is also a worrying loss in what had seemed a more or less safely ordered world.

When the young adolescent's body is no longer child-like, then touch and reassurance can seem less safe, for them and for their parents. Some of the inevitable tensions of need, resentment and rivalry are illustrated in the following observation.

> On a summer evening at a rock concert in the park, a 12-year-old girl in all her pubescent excitement and anxiety was with her parents.
>
> **Daisy** was slightly plump, bursting with hormones and her newly sexual body, all set to try her seductive powers on her father.
>
> She stood close to him, turning her full gaze on him. She played the 'broken egg' game on him, play-cracking the *egg* on his skull with her fingers as *yolk*, running down his hair and neck. She asked him to do the same to her. He did so.
>
> Daisy repeated the game, again asking her father to crack the egg over her. Her father smiled and looked away, attempting to engage his wife in the game, too: she looked at him rather crossly – and turned away.
>
> Daisy again cracked the egg over her father, looking at him, giggling and running her hands down his neck. Her father turned again to his wife,

cracking an egg over her and laughing. Daisy's mother smiled and seemed more lively; Daisy seemed at a loss, but she joined in the laughter, mother and daughter looking at each other warily. She then cracked the egg over her mother – and turned again to her father.

Her mother broke an egg over Daisy, the parents giggling. Daisy looked at her mother with cold fury. As soon as her parents broke apart, she shone her eyes at her father, smiling at him and excluding her mother, who looked away.

Daisy rumpled her father's hair and he rumpled hers. She smoothed her hair carefully – and he rumpled it again. Daisy was laughing – but also annoyed. Her father invited the mother in to rumple Daisy's hair, which she did. Mother and daughter stared at each other, laughing – and hostile.

The scene continued . . .

Daisy needed reassurance that she was loved, and that her newly sexual body was desirable. But responding to a seductive adolescent daughter, without being too close or withdrawing too far, is difficult and disturbing for many men without the help of an involved mother – and Daisy's father kept looking for his wife's support.

Somehow. Daisy's mother had got shut out: maybe she gave up too quickly and handed her daughter over to the father. We cannot know. But triumphing over a denigrated mother is not a stable basis on which to build a sense of self-worth for a young girl or boy. Daisy actually needs her mother's help and support to make her flirtatious games with her father safely boundaried – but her intense hostility to her mother (and her mother's withdrawal) make this less likely.

An adolescent needs to find a way of establishing an independent relationship with a parent, but really challenging, disagreeing and standing their ground might risk leaving a parent collapsed, or hostile. And when *challenge* becomes a cover for excited, withering *contempt*, a parent can be hard-put to resist feeling deflated, infuriated, or both. If Daisy's parents can resist being pulled apart by their daughter's seductiveness and rivalry, then she will find there are limits to her excited powers – but she will be less guilty that she has triumphed over and deprived her mother, whose support and love would be helpful to her. Having parents (whether they live together or not) who can manage a disagreement as part of everyday life without its being a *calamity* is very helpful to the young person.

Daisy seems to be seeking to find confidence by seeing herself as desirable, and sexually desirable, in a man's eyes. But if that is her only way to find reassurance, she risks becoming sexually vulnerable. For her own well-being, she needs to be able to protect herself and notice her limits so that, at her own steady pace (rather than the pace determined by her anxious need for affirmation) she can venture out into the adult world.

Gender

Prior to puberty, gender might not have felt like a pressing problem. Until that time children can feel themselves to be both, or neither; they can have friends of both sexes.

With the approach of puberty and its bodily changes, most adolescents feel confused and anxious, as well as excited. They are losing the body they had, the person they felt themself to be. They are becoming an adult: one gender and not the other. And what sort of man or woman are they supposed to become?

Many adolescent boys will feel excited by becoming more *manly*, in his penis and its erections, and that can become a focus for him and his excited banter with peers. He can also feel an expectation to be masculine as a burden. He *should* feel brave, daring and in charge – but what if he feels shy and hesitant instead? What if he wants to feel playful (not in a manly one-up kind of way), or enjoys giving and receiving attention reciprocally (rather than proving how impressive he is)? Is he allowed to feel tender, sensitive or loving? Does not being the *biggest* at everything, mean that he *fails*?

And what of girls? If, in former generations, they were expected to be responsive to others and their needs, and this is now less extreme, in early adolescence girls still face a disturbing expectation of how their body *should* be. The dolls latency girls play with and dress generally have an artificially thin waist, flat belly, blonde hair and high heels, without which she cannot stand up. This glamorous model is, by definition, unattainable.

> In one experiment, girls of 9 or 10 were given a doll similar to a Barbie but with proportions similar to a young teenage girl with plumper thighs and belly and with brown hair. The girls responded that the doll was 'like me' or 'like my sister' and was felt to be 'kind', an attribute not connected to Barbie. When given the choice of keeping this doll or being given a Barbie, the girls mostly voted for the doll felt to be more like her. (Though they may still not have wanted to give up *all* their Barbies.) (Lamm, 2014).

If the expected standard is that of Barbie and air-brushed models, then bodily, the girl is a *failure*. Must she fit in with other expectations, and if so, which ones? What if she wants to be noisy or naughty?

Gains from feminism of the 1960s and 1970s achieved a much wider acceptance of how a woman or a man can be. Gay rights and same-sex marriage expanded the room for expression of less gendered stereotypes. At puberty, most are able to find room for a version of themselves as gendered without feeling unbearably straitjacketed. Still, some young adolescents feel that their genitals do not fit: they are in the wrong body.

For some, feeling their body to be *wrong* can be associated with difficulty in their earlier relationships. Some feel that the child their parents wanted was not them, but one of the other sex, or another child who has died. A child who has been abused, or witnessed abuse, can want to alter that body and make it anew. A child who has not been able to mourn a lost, loved figure can try to represent them in their altered body (Welldon, 1989; McDougall, 1995; Ehrensaft, 2007; Di Ceglie, 2009, 2014; Lemma, 2012.Some have felt this from an early age, as a fixed belief. In some cases there seems to be a biological contribution and a suggested link to autistic symptoms (Di Ceglie, 2014).

Children and adolescents at the Tavistock Gender Identity Service, and their parents, can be helped to resist a rush into action but to tolerate the uncertainty; to discover more conscious access to their feelings and experiences, rather than everything being expressed through the body. Whether or not that adolescent goes on to pursue hormonal treatment and surgery, they can accept themselves more and mourn the loss of the perfect body they might wish for. About one third go on to gender reassignment; others feel able to accept themselves and their bodies as they are, gender fluid (Di Ceglie & Freedman, 1998; Di Ceglie, 2008, 2014).

Relations with friends

As ties with parents loosen, so the peer group becomes increasingly important.

Fiercely loving and possessive feelings, ones of rivalry and hostility as well as tender ones, are explored newly with friends. There is a powerful pressure to fit in – or else be excluded. Physicality and aggression can be expressed in fights. Boys in particular can move to a mocking aggression as a way of keeping away any tender feelings. Girls may feel more safely allowed to hug, be affectionate and to discuss heartaches, but hostility can be expressed more indirectly in bullying and ganging up on one who is made the outsider.

With friends we may learn to disagree and stand up for ourselves. We try out different versions of ourselves. Having someone to confide in can be an enormous relief. We might be anxious and insecure, but we aren't alone in this worrying state.

Having friends means that we can experiment with a sexual partner without the driven need for company and reassurance. We are not looking for one person to fill every single need – and then if they are lost it is not a complete disaster. There are still familiar faces, there for us. We learn that we need to care for them back, or we lose them.

When it is hard to have or maintain friendships, then it is possible to withdraw increasingly into a fantasy world. Masturbation can be a relief. Computer screens offer distractions and different ways of playing out realities. Facebook offers an opportunity to present a carefully scripted version of yourself – but still there is that miserable gap from what real human contact may offer.

In early adolescence you can long to be physically held and reassured – and this is mixed in confusingly with sexual stirrings. Desires and fantasies in relation to friends can be troubling: what if you find your friend's body alluring, whether the same or the opposite sex?

Freud pointed out that there is an inevitable bisexuality in both girls and in boys: wanting exclusive possession of the mother of infancy (as well as hostility), and parallel feelings of love, possessiveness and wishes to be like (as well as hostility towards) their father. He thought that boys and young men were more likely to disavow more nurturing 'feminine' feelings in themselves due to social pressures. These constraints are shifting and some young men of the present generation feel more at ease acknowledging tender feelings.

Many adolescents experiment with same-sex encounters, some on their way towards a heterosexual partnering, and others not. Emotionally, bodily, a same-sex partner can feel less alarmingly unfamiliar. Being with a same-sex partner may allow more possibilities of how to be, less at risk of falling into the demands of stereotyped sexual roles.

It can also be a response to difficulties in early relationships with parents. For the boy, if his mother and women are felt as engulfing, then a same-sex partner can be less burdened with fears of over-closeness, and resentment. For a girl, if men are seen as only useless, absent or threateningly hostile, then she may turn towards another woman to fulfil her desires for sex and love.

Acknowledging loving and sexual feelings towards someone of the same sex has become more acceptable and such wishes are less confused than they once were with being outcast and fear of punishment (as well as sometimes the excitement of the forbidden and the shocking).

But same-sex or not, exploring sexual and emotional intimacy still means managing fears of being exposed or dependent; feelings of possessive love and jealous hatred; of difference and vulnerability.

Being cool

Coolness looks like an appealing way to manage feelings of gawkiness, embarrassment and a dread of failure. It can start early:

> **Leon**, observed in a special needs class, was 12. His parents, who had found education hard themselves, could not reassure him that struggles and mistakes were an inevitable part of learning and did not mean he was stupid. So Leon managed his feelings of humiliation at being slower than his classmates by looking as cool as he could, with slicked-back hair, a white leather jacket with tassels, and a careless slouch.

Leon was forming a tight protective shell around himself. He was making himself cool, macho: challenging and fun maybe. Still, we might worry for Leon that if he keeps on in this way, it will be hard for him in the future to let anyone in to help when it risks his vulnerabilities being seen and mocked – just as he so mocked himself.

If the young adolescent boy or girl cannot find a way to tolerate tender, possessive and vulnerable feelings, then it becomes almost impossible to have a relationship that is close.

The following youngsters are lucky, in that they have found a way to express the difficulty.

> At a warm, boisterous youth camp, a group of 13-year-olds were putting on a skit on Romeo and Juliet. What they said openly mirrored the cool, sexualized culture: but they followed this with the echo of an *uncool* version, lying behind.
>
> So the young Romeo addresses the girl:
>
> *You look hot, I wouldn't mind giving you some action.*
>
> She responds, feistily, in kind. But the hidden subtext is one of gentleness and vulnerability – when Romeo quietly says,
>
> *You're so lovely. I'd love to touch your cheek. How can I say anything that won't make me look stupid?*

Chapter 14

Late adolescence

In the classic American children's story, *The Runaway Bunny*, a little bunny threatens to run away, leave his mother and hide in all kinds of disguises – as a fish, a crocus, a bird, a boy ... Each time his mother tells him how she will find him and hold him in her arms. Finally, he gives in:

> "Shucks" said the bunny, "I might just as well stay where I am and be your little bunny".
> And so he did.
> "Have a carrot" said the mother bunny.
>
> (Wise Brown, 1942)

The story is touching and reassuring both for the little bunny listening and for his (or her) parent.

But the time comes for the late adolescent to really fly away, find out for himself the dangers in the outside world, and test his resources to cope with them. (And the job of a parent is no longer to *catch him in her arms* but to let him go. In doing so, that parent has to manage feelings of her or his own – which are likely to include loss and sadness, hurt and anger at being turned away from with such excitement, and jealousy, as well as pleasure and relief – such that arms can still be held warmly open when the sometimes still needy young adult returns.)

Late adolescence brings all the challenges of leaving childhood, bearing being alone some of the time, finding out who you are, risking sex and intimacy. This is tough enough for any adolescent, but even harder to the degree that conflict and difficulty has been evaded earlier on.

Leaving home

Living in the family home, it is possible to take for granted all kinds of care, which happens almost unnoticed. Being away from the structure a family provides, the routine domestic maintenance but also the emotional caring and company (however imperfect and resented), can be a surprising shock.

Winnicott spoke of the child who learns to be alone and absorbed in his own activities with the background unobtrusive presence of his mother or other carer (1958). She creates the safe setting: he is not abandoned, left all alone with his impulses and anxieties, and this allows him the freedom to be absorbed in his own discoveries and to play. He is alone but not lonely. Or when he becomes so, then he can reach out, knowing that he has a particular need.

For someone whose earlier experience was of emotionally unavailable, unconnected parenting, then he might hang around with others, but in a disconnected way, or might frantically scramble for company, but in a conflicted way, since his expectations of contact is of disappointment or danger.

If you can't bear being alone some of the time and have to just rush round, then you have no time and space to know your own mind. But if reaching out seems too needy, then it's possible to become increasingly isolated:

> **Steve** was a very able boy in an academic school who felt that he should excel at everything he turned his hand to. Rather like his mother, he was dismissive of his successful, but modest, father. He hated being teased or seen as having anything to learn. Chatting up girls felt horribly exposing and he withdrew into a cool arrogance and waited for them to approach him.
>
> In his first weeks at university, Steve felt in a flat panic. He felt too anxious and foolish to talk to anyone but instead looked on scornfully at the others, frantically chatting.
>
> At home, when he withdrew, his mother would come looking for him, as had his teachers at school. Now no one seemed to notice. Steve felt frightened and lonely: smoking dope helped his growing sense of desperation, but made it even harder to make contact with anyone.
>
> He went home for the weekend, fighting feelings of desperate failure – and could not bring himself to go back again.

Steve's pattern of managing his anxiety by ignoring it and being effortlessly superior had worked so well up till this point but now, entering the outside world, he felt woefully ill-equipped. He had not yet learned to tolerate feeling small or hungry without being overwhelmed with hatred and self-hatred.

When it is not possible to acknowledge needs and anxiety, they can be managed indirectly.

> When the pregnancy test read positive **Debby** had a sinking feeling. She knew she had taken a risk but thought, at that time of month, it would be all right. A bit of her was excited: she loved babies! It might even be a relief in that having a baby would solve the problem of what to do when she left the safe familiarity of college.
>
> Logically, she knew it was mad: she was 20; she knew she wasn't going to stay with the father, and having the baby alone would be mad, too.

Debby had an abortion and felt very low; she picked up an infection and came home to her family to get a bit of 'babying' for herself. With her parents' support she began to feel better and had some hope of forgiving herself.

Is it possible that Debby, in not recognizing her anxieties sufficiently, allowed herself to 'accidentally' get pregnant, *having* a baby rather than *being* (if temporarily) a baby? If so, then learning to recognize her own needs consciously and attending to them directly would be an important part of growing up.

Growing up can also involve having to take back as valuable what had previously been sneered at.

Jane would scoff at her father's anxiety about getting anywhere on time: she felt excitedly superior to his over-carefulness.

When she left home and no longer had her father to push her, Jane missed several planes and trains. It was as if somewhere she had a belief that she was so special that the planes would wait for her, as her parents might have once done. She discovered that she needed an *anxious father* bit of herself, noticing that delays can happen, to counterbalance that superior teenage her.

Sex

We bring such high expectations of what a sexual encounter should be like and how we should be, too. Sex is sold as the best thing ever. Sex can seem to offer a shortcut to closeness, touch and connection – yet the reality of it can be disappointing and alienating.

Sex stirs up so much of what is infantile. It may be exciting – but it is also disturbing. Bodily, it is probably the closest we have been to another person since infancy. Caught up in the sway of urgent physical sensations with few words, barely under the control of any rational, logical adult self, we are touched and held as otherwise we are not. Seen intimately by another, we are at our most vulnerable, naked in all its aspects: our body and its longings are open for scrutiny, which might feel critical as well as appreciative.

Film, fiction and pornography can convey what a perfect sexual relationship *should be* and anything less than that can feel shameful. You can be left feeling that you have to please not only your partner, but also a critic in your head who is observing your body and its responses. And that interferes with the possibility of safely enjoying pleasure.

Once, social pressure and fear of pregnancy led to extended periods of chastity, which could be protective as well as frustrating. Now the pressure is to be sexually active and fulfilled, whether in a close relationship or not, whether liking, trusting – or even being particularly interested in – the other person.

For the teenage boy, a woman's body and her breasts (in the distant past such a source of fascination, desire and, later, renunciation) is a source of conflict. He might be anxious about the idea of a female partner, her interior genitals, and fear being trapped – physically and emotionally. He might dread that he could be pulled into something too infantile, stirring up dependency needs and resentments last felt in relation to his mother and then he may need to keep his distance from a woman. Getting close to a woman, or recognizing any need for her, can feel just too threatening.

He could worry that he might damage a partner as a result of his frustrated furies as well as his excited hunger, whose source is in the past as well as in the present. He might resent her potential fecundity. And if he cannot allow himself to risk being cared for, then he has few resources to be caring in turn.

The teenage girl's attitude towards her female body will affect her feelings towards a partner. As well as feeling curiosity, she might resent or fear a potential partner's penis and what it represents. She might have fears about what sort of man and what sort of penis she will take inside her, and wish to control or deflate any excitement evident in him.

When sex feels too exposing emotionally, it can feel safer to shut down feelings and have the experience as just a 'screw', a notch on the belt. A partner who stirs up longings can feel threatening, and it can feel safer to withdraw. Feeling vulnerable with a sexual partner, it is tempting to denigrate them before they do you.

Pornography

Compared to sex with another person, pornography can feel a welcome relief. You don't need to feel anxious or uncertain. You are in control: no longer open to scrutiny and judgement.

The one in the image invites you in. The one depicted is no longer a person in their own right but they are partial: their large breasts, their toned muscles, their displayed genitals. Pornography can express feelings which otherwise feel shameful. You may be sexually excited but it is not to do with care for, or even noticing, that other person, but about being powerful, and maybe cruel or submitting to a cruel them.

When such feelings are apparently encouraged and normalized, it can conflict disturbingly with any more tender impulses towards a sexual partner. And if we have such excited depersonalizing feelings towards them, then what about theirs towards us?

If we can't allow someone to really *see* us, then it is harder to let them be close. We need to have made some rough peace with ourselves.

When there have been earlier difficulties in feeling loved and loving, then the task of moving into a more adult world is particularly hard. When hostile barriers have been set up to protect against vulnerability, then it can feel that we are a danger to others and they to us.

Feelings including hurt, self-doubt and hatred stopped 15-year-old **Ollie** from reaching out to peers. He felt that others, particularly girls, were contemptuous of him, and this made him withdraw into himself more. He came reluctantly into therapy at the suggestion of a teacher at his sixth-form college.

Ollie's mother had left home when he was 8 and did not maintain contact with him. His father found a new partner. For several years Ollie remained with them and their new family, feeling superior – but also left out. He then lived with his grandmother.

The male analyst noticed how, when he came to leave the session, Ollie expressed fear and contempt. The analyst felt that he was being shown something of the pain of feeling worthless and unwanted – as Ollie must have felt, and feel still, at his mother's abandoning him. He took this up in one way or another over months and also how Ollie, in pulling contemptuously away, added to his feeling alone and unwanted.

Ollie began to think about his hatred for his mother who had left him, and his dread that she had left because of his angry demands of her. As a result of such feelings becoming more thinkable, Ollie found that he would like to meet his mother.

When he did, he was astonished to find that his mother was not the cruel, unloving figure that he had assumed: she had been depressed, felt guilty for leaving her young son and feared that he would never forgive her.

Ollie was astonished: even though she had abandoned him, his mother had continued to think of him. She had loved him! This was a ground-shifting discovery for him.

Ollie was pleased to notice that he had concerned feelings for his mother, not only ones of hurt and hatred. He wanted to stay in touch with her, for her sake but also for his own. He felt less toxic.

Ollie had managed a very painful situation externally, by turning away. His confidence was still fragile, but he began to feel that he had more of a basis to reach out to others, girls in particular, and hope that they would not just despise or hate him. He was able to risk letting his guard down.

In love

Being *in love* recreates the hoped-for bliss of our earliest days with a mother (or a father), held in their adoring gaze, in their mind and their arms, seen and wanted.

In that infantile part of mind we can all wish that a partner or a dear friend would be like that wished-for, doting parent of infancy: attentive to our needs with apparently no other needs of their own, wanting them to find us lovable in every way, even when we know we are not and when, rationally, we know this is unreasonable. Most of us hope that a new love will right all past wrongs and deprivations: a loved one's love and devotion will make everything endlessly all right. And when inevitably, it does not, just like that first Oedipal blow, then there is loss, disillusionment and rage.

A couple who become more intimate and committed, no longer only sexually hungry, have to manage conflicts to do with separateness and feelings of exclusion, rivalry and fear of loss that are an inevitable in being a part of a loving couple – and yet still separate.

Allowing the other to matter

> *Are you here for just one day and tomorrow take it away*
> *Oh baby, be for real won't you baby*
> *because I don't want to be hurt by love again . . .*
> *if it's a thrill you're looking for, honey I can be flexible . . .*
> (Frederick Knight, and sung by Leonard Cohen)

In past generations there was little escape from a commitment once made. Today, sexual engagements are made earlier, and separations are frequent – which makes loving a partner more risky.

If you cannot bear to manage the possible pain of being so thrilled and hopeful, in love, and then being disappointed, then it will be hard to allow another really close. Longing for closeness and intimacy can feel too wounding.

Cynicism, being *flexible*, you hope, can protect you against pain at the loss of the beloved. It is as though love can only be risked if there is a guarantee. But mostly when entering into a relationship, neither knows yet what is *for real* and what is not, or for how long. Only time, inevitable hurt and disillusion can resolve that.

Wishing for closeness can stir up feelings of anxiety and self-disgust. It can feel much safer to have such risky feelings as love or longing in our partner than in ourself. But those who continue such a course can find it increasingly isolating and bleak. A shut-down, self-protective love may look safer – but puts stress on a partnership and makes an ending more likely:

> Though in his thirties, **Mark** brought difficulties he had not yet found a way to solve from his teenage (and earlier) years.
>
> He longed for a partner. But he was burdened by hateful feelings from the past: rage at his mother (and his father) for producing a baby brother when he was 3 and leaving him feeling left out and punished for his furious protests, which he could never quite let go of. He had not found a way to manage that early Oedipal blow of life, development and sometimes exclusion. Its impact continued.
>
> Mark's chronic feeling was of being badly treated, resentful, and desperately longing to be loved. But he could not believe that anyone with any

value could love him. He hated his mother for having abandoned her promise of an exclusive bond with him, as her best partner and baby. And he hated women for the hurt, humiliation and rejection he feared from them. So he turned the tables on them, becoming aloof and superior. A woman who did put up with his attacks, Mark despised. When one did not and left, he felt gutted and even more full of self-hatred.

The miserable spiral continued.

All couples have to find their way round the pain of managing separateness, and of allowing closeness and intimacy that leave both vulnerable to hurt and loss. One way is to find a relationship that is safe but which doesn't challenge us as much as we might otherwise wish.

Connie had been with her boyfriend Tim for three years. They'd met at college, had some time apart, made trips together: they were good buddies, but Connie wasn't sure that was enough. Sometimes she felt more like Tim's big sister and wanted to give him a shake. She loved him and knew he'd be a good father and would never leave her (which concerned her, as her parents had broken up, bitterly).

But the thought of the next 30 years or more together dismayed her. She thought if Tim wanted to please her it was more to keep the peace, rather than really caring for her and wanting her best interests as well as his own.

She worried about hurting Tim if she left; she worried about being lonely and whether she would ever find someone better matched. She wasn't sure how much the difficulty was Tim's – or was she just difficult to please?

Connie was wondering whether she could risk finding someone more equal who really mattered to her but, were the relationship to go wrong, would leave her vulnerable to hurt and loss. There would be losses as well as gains whatever Connie decided – and part of growing up may be in finding that there is rarely a perfect, painless answer.

Part IV

Adulthood

The tasks of adulthood mean being able to attend not only to our own self-interest but to others' as well. To wish not only to be loved and admired, but to find a capacity to value, protect and love - in intimate relationships over the long-term, under the stresses of parenthood, and those with whom we work.

Disappointments and disillusionment need to be born. Differences and dis-agreements need to be negotiated without turning to hatred, victimhood and blame. And this is not easy.

Chapter 15

Love

Life at my age is not easy, but spring is beautiful and so is love.
(Freud at 80 to poet and former patient, H.D. (H.D., 1970, p. 194))

Feeling that particular others matter to you and you to them makes life feel worthwhile – and its lack can feel very bleak. Having a partnership or loving friendships makes the world feel a safer place: loved ones are a buffer against disappointments and losses, which we inevitably face. While those losses may be desperately sad they will not be *devastating* – in that there remains some hope that there is still love, *beauty*, in the world and within us. All has not been utterly demolished.

To the extent that we are less able to allow others in, for fear of being found unlovable, we carry a heavy, lonely burden. We are more likely to feel aggrieved, resentful, envious and, therefore, in a vicious spiral, less lovable.

We may all hope to be loved and loving but the reality is often much more complicated. Loving, even with friends, is not always easy and the same old problems of frustration, disappointments, envy and jealousy all have to be re-negotiated.

We can wish that a perfect partner will be ever loving, ever-fresh, ever-supportive, there for us when we want them – though not bringing their own demands when we do not. We may know how important other relationships are for us in terms of support, stimulation, a change of view, the pleasure of groupings and partnerships of all kinds – but still at some hidden level resent a partner who has pleasure away from us. Old feelings can be stirred up of hurt, fear of loss and of missing, and then of frustration, rage and envy.

> **Susie**'s husband Dan sometimes would have to stay overnight on business. Susie did not worry that he was having an affair: she knew that he needed to be away, she even quite enjoyed having the evening to herself – but she was furious at the thought that he might have any pleasure in being away from her.

On his return, Susie would be cold and sulky for days. She felt like a jealous toddler. She knew it was ridiculous, but she felt she *should not be treated like this*. If anyone was going to feel left out and longing for closeness it should be Dan, not her.

There is still that bit of most of us that, at some level, wants to claim that we are the centre of the universe and it is others' job to fit in around us. We should not have to acknowledge another's separateness, their feelings, their flaws, their history, their vulnerabilities, as well as all that is lovable and enviable in them. They should not need our love and support: any attention and feeding should be one way. We can want them to be like the teddy bear of childhood: bearing with our tyrannies without complaint. These feelings can coexist with other, more loving, generous ones.

Noticing the impact our demands have on our loved one, their hurt anger and exhaustion, then we face guilt. It might help to change our behaviour. To the degree we cannot or will not bear such discomfort, then we can rack up the intensity of our denial and demanding submission to keep increasing guilt at bay. We might attack the loved one in our minds and in our actions. But this can be increasingly fraught.

To allow someone close, to really see us, we need to have made some peace with ourselves. To the degree that we haven't, we will cover over and protect from fear of being found out and rejected. Those whose experiences of parenting and care are less robust, whose self-worth is fragile and potential loss is too threatening, it can feel too difficult to risk hope and hurt. It is not surprising if we enter into relationship crab-like, stepping sideways and not quite knowing where it will all end up.

Winning the Oedipal battle can seem exciting and gratifying – but it can get in the way of later adult loving relationships, or becoming a parent oneself:

> **Claire**, now a bright academic, had always loved intellectual conversations with her father: she and he were the special couple. A part of the pleasure was that her mother, whom she saw as rather stupid, was left out.
>
> As a teenager and young adult Claire fell in love with a series of married men, whom she idealized and she felt a familiar quiet superiority towards her lovers' wives and children. It worked well for a long time: Claire felt excited, alive, desired.
>
> She was painfully aware that she would like to find a long-term partner and might even want a child, but this would be dangerous, for then she would be in the position of her despised mother, and at risk of being triumphed over by another (younger) woman.
>
> In her analysis, Claire treated her woman analyst in a subtly dismissive way, rather as if she was doing her analyst a favour in coming – and this her

analyst pointed out. Slowly, often as a result of noticing how things were in her relationship with her analyst (in the transference), dreams and memories came to mind.

In the third year of her analysis, one memory suddenly flooded back of having once *adored* her mother. Claire wanted to ridicule this strange new thought: probably she was just tired or needed a good break, or some good sex. But she knew somehow that it was true, even if it overturned all the assumptions by which she had lived her life. It was a shocking thought for her that somehow, in her rivalry and jealousy, she had devalued her mother. She felt ashamed, guilty and grief-stricken.

Claire began to feel closer to her mother. Her relationship with her partner deepened and settled and she began to feel safe enough to think that she might become a mother in her turn.

Need

> *If you tame me, then we shall need each other ... if you tame me, it will be as if the sun came to shine on my life. I shall know the sound of a step that will be different from all the others*
>
> (St Exupery, 2012).

The idea of needing another can seem disturbing and unsafe. Independence, toughness and cool can look admirable, but leaves you at a distance, undisturbed for good, but also for the bad.

When feelings of longing or need are hard to bear, it can seem easier to stimulate desire in another. Your partner, family member, friend or work colleague may be interested in all that you have to offer, but nevertheless sense that in all this activity, somehow, you are not fully interested in *them*, their being *different from all the others*. The ability to feel moved by another, to mind if they leave, to care for them rather than only their capacity to care for you, can leave you worryingly vulnerable – but if you can't allow that, then how can you really love or be loved?

Acknowledging need in yourself also requires recognizing what the loved other has that is desirable and enviable. It can be tempting to evade issues such as envy and Oedipal exclusion, but it can have a sad impact.

> **Stan** had grown up feeling very special, with a very close relationship to his adored mother, and rather looking down on his working-class father. He gained a place at a prestigious university, met and married Em, a warm professional woman and, in time, they had a child.
>
> It was painful to Stan that Em did not centre her whole world round him as his mother had done and he minded her involvement with their son: if anyone should have the special relationship it was him, not Em. Logically, he knew he was being stupid – but this did not change his feeling.

When Stan's mother died he felt angry at his mother for leaving him; angry that she had worn herself out and died younger than she might; angry at Em, who still had her mother, and whose preoccupation with her mother's ill-health meant that Em was not as available for him as he wanted.

Stan started an affair with someone who admired and needed him much more than he felt Em did. He excitedly planned to leave but then, to his surprise, he felt panicked. With his mother alive, the need had always been *his mother's* for him, her adored special son – flattering and sometimes cloying. For the first time, Stan began to see that *he* might have needed his mother, just as he did Em. He had not appreciated her.

If Stan can hold on to this awareness, he might then sadly mourn and feel grief and guilt: he might worry whether his demands on his mother added to wearing her out.

Were he to do so, then he may be more able to make warmer relations with women, less needing to be the only one with goods, whether he managed to do so with Em or with a new partner. In giving up his demand to be 'his Majesty the baby', he would be more adult: able to have an ordinarily passionate, companionable, reciprocal relationship with his partner and able to parent his son, rather than rival him – at least some of the time.

Tolerating dependence

Another way of not noticing care given is to be apparently the constant provider. This can look admirably giving and self-sacrificing, but it can cover up an anxiety about being in the vulnerable position of wanting and receiving care. And for a partner, that can be distancing and alienating.

You may snatch care on the quiet but you cannot openly take pleasure in being cared for, or ask for what you need. And the other, deprived of the pleasure in feeling that the care they offer is valued, is likely to start offering less.

> When **Paul** was 4, his mother was in hospital with a life-threatening illness. Afterwards, he seemed very good but he was passive and distant. Later, as an adult in analysis, he recognized how he had determined never to let his mother close again.
>
> When he married, he looked like the perfect husband, heroically putting up with a wife who seemed to be demanding and unreasonable. Puzzlingly, just at the moment Paul might have left, he had unprotected sex with his wife, who got pregnant.
>
> What only became clear as it unfolded in the transference relation with his woman analyst was how subtly provocative Paul was, stirring up her interest and concern – and then withdrawing. He was nudging her to become exasperated and controlling.

Noticing this, Paul could begin to wonder whether this same thing had happened with his mother and with his wife; whether it might be a relief to have a demanding partner, to whom he could feel superior, one who was reassuringly present, nagging him – not leaving him or dying. And in a part of his mind Paul believed that if his wife were to die, he would feel relieved, not devastated.

His view of his wife became softer.

Allowing someone to look after you, and feeling grateful offers reassurance to the provider: their gifts are noticed and valued. The situation then is less of scarce resources that you have to hold on to tightly for fear of loss, but offers the possibilities of replenishment, by receiving care and having more inside to offer care in turn.

Sex in an ongoing relationship

A sexual encounter, even if it was not intended as a loving one, can stir up all kinds of primitive, excited feelings that you might not have anticipated which are not only adult, sexual ones, but also ones which are passionately infantile. It stirs up feelings of dependence and longing which are a part of the excited in love phase.

When a partnership starts to settle, with your loved one (and you) known in your worst as well as your best moments, such intense feelings can feel too dangerous. There is a safety in making that loved one matter less, not only out of familiarity, but also out of envy and dread of loss – even if it makes the partnership more disappointing and the temptations to look elsewhere greater (Mitchell, 2003).

> **Bill** was settled in a long and, more or less, happy marriage. He felt he would be *boring* if he did not respond to the flirtation of a work colleague. But the encounter stirred up astonishingly much in him.
>
> It wasn't that the sex in itself was so brilliant, though the experience of an unfamiliar body and its responses to him was intoxicating. In one way Bill felt as he had as an excited 18-year old. He also felt as he might have as a little baby with his mother: with someone who held him, listened to him, made him feel as if he were the only one, not only one to be fitted in between a hectic life and all its demands.
>
> He felt a fury that that special him had been ignored and taken for granted by his wife for all those years – just as he had taken her for granted, too.

Arguably as important as the particular choice that any of us might make is how we live with the particular decision and make it work for the best.

> **Angie** had had an early passionate relationship, which broke up and left her agonized.

As her pain at its ending slowly settled, she could see that a man such as her ex, flamboyant and needing so much attention for himself, would never be an easy one to live with long term or have a family with. She decided that being the support act to one who always wanted to be in the starring role was less exciting than it had looked at first sight.

A dear friend, Pete, became her lover and she appreciated him more and more. Angie married Pete and, 15 years later, was still pleased that she had done so. She felt loved and loving.

Angie could have made the same choice but with lingering regret, in a second-best, superior sort of way – and made the happy outcome much less likely. As much as the choice she made, what was important was the way she committed herself fully to her decision, allowing her partner to really matter to her.

Freud was not speaking of only romantic or sexual love, but of a capacity to *be loving*. Actively loving someone is a very different thing to the delight of being loved, or of being in love, when your loved one seems so perfect.

We are most of us at our happiest when we feel loving and when we feel ourselves loved. Being known in our good moments and in the bad, and still cared for, is an astonishing relief. Trust in the loved one grows and we are able to risk opening up more and offering more. We are no longer only in the presence of a combatant, a rival or a judge.

If hurts and anger are too dangerous to express, then closeness can feel more like a caricature than the real thing. Only by finding out whether a relationship can survive disagreement do you have the opportunity to find out whether you both are more robust than you feared. It may then feel freer – but there is still no avoiding the task of negotiating inevitable moments of painful frustration, envy and jealousy.

Allowing ourself to be more open, letting loved ones have full value, has many pleasures. We want to protect and care for those important, loved ones; we may also find ourself concerned for others beyond our immediate circle: wanting to look after and fight for others and for the world we leave to the next generation.

Chapter 16

Parenting

The arrival of their first born is often an unimaginable shock for a couple. As well as delight and pleasure, there is the anxiety of caring for this new baby, sheer exhaustion and loss of time for each individual, let alone for the two as a couple. Many new parents wearily feel that they have suddenly become serfs to the demands of their new baby, who allows them to sleep – or not.

As well as physical demands there are emotional ones too.

Oedipus and parents

Freud emphasized the second part of the Oedipus story.[1] It is worth noting the first part, too:

> Oedipus's father, Laius, found it intolerable that his baby son had the passionate love of his wife and would in time *best* him (by growing up, as Laius grew old). He wanted his wife to agree to send away their son to his presumed death, so that he could have her to himself again.

When a couple become parents and that twosome which had seemed to work so well suddenly becomes a three, Oedipal feelings of exclusion and jealousy are poignantly stirred up. A father may well struggle with his wish to support his partner and her new love-interest, the baby, for his own (infantile as well as adult) needs for her have been shut out by this rival – especially if the newcomer is a boy (Emanuel, 2002). He may resent and punish his rival in quiet or in noisy ways.

He can want to compete with the mother to be the best parent to the new baby; he can deprive her and withdraw – and if she is exhausted and resentful, he can feel, in some part, that it serves her right.

> The arrival of their first baby stirred up early feelings for **Sean** of being left out as a 1-year old by his mother when she'd had another baby. Just as he had suffered then and hated the new baby and his mother in her pleasure, so as an adult he struggled with such feelings.

Sean withdrew. When he saw his partner struggle, he felt some guilty pleasure and relief: she was no longer the woman he had fallen in love with.

Some years later, the marriage was in trouble. Sean was driven partly by guilt: he did not want to face the partner who now so resented him for his withdrawal. He felt hopeless, too: if he were to notice his part and wish to make things better, it would leave him vulnerable – and she might not want him even then. If his children suffered, in a part of his mind he felt that they deserved it, taking his special place as they had. Sean also hoped that with his new partner he could do better next time.

In the years that followed, Sean did his best to not notice the sad impact on his children. He did his best not to miss them in his daily life, or feel regret: he made himself busy and told himself that life was great. And then he became very depressed.

Finally (and with some analytic help), he began to acknowledge some of these things: he could see how much the arrival of the new baby when he was so very little had left him wanting to muscle out any rivals and grab what attention was available. Noticing how this had impacted on his marriage and his children, he felt shocked, guilty and very sad: he had not protected who and what he had loved.

But he felt less on a perpetual spin. He was able to make a better relationship with his now adult children.

A mother, too, has the delight (as well as the exhaustion) of being the centre of her new baby's world. This can gratify her own wishes to be the one and only. To the degree that she has resentments of her partner (as well as those which stem from her own early history), she can gain satisfaction in turning away from her partner. She can be reluctant to help him have his own special relation with the baby, when it means she is no longer the only special one, some of the time no longer the one who is best.

To the degree that we still have old resentments of parents who did not provide everything and who left us out, it can feel hard to be a parent ourselves who is anything less than perfect and loving. As if by parenting so perfectly, we might show those flawed parents of our childhood their failure in matching up to such a standard.

There is immense pleasure when the baby settles, and reassures his anxious parents that they do have good things to offer. But often for a new parent there is a dismaying gap between what expectations of how mothers, babies and fathers should be and the reality that there are other moments when the baby just will not settle.

Suddenly, an exhausted mother (or father) can find herself frustrated and furious with her baby: *why can't he see how hard I am trying! Why can't he just grow up!* – and be ashamed that such feelings may make her a bad mother. Just like the bad and still unforgiven mother (or father) of childhood.

When we identify overly with the baby's rage, we may give in to keep the short-term peace, but then feel even more resentful, and then guilty. Then it can be hard to be enjoyably part of a parental couple that leaves the baby ever *outside*. We will have to give more and more, and get more and more depleted until we finally explode, and then that rage is much more frightening. Or we can turn that rage on ourselves for being bad and become depressed.

Feeling guilty and resenting a baby who seems to be so demanding, one way of managing is to turn away and be less emotionally available to our growing child – which leaves him in considerable distress.

Old resentments and Oedipal competition to be the best loved by the baby can interfere with parents supporting each other in the tough task of parenting.

It is so helpful for a mother when her partner is able to support her in looking after the baby, and to remind her that her baby's reality is only a partial one: the baby may be in a panic and rage if his mother leaves, but babies don't die from frustration and fury. A partner who is on the mother's side can reassure her when their baby refuses to be soothed and can remind her that she is not a useless mother. It helps a mother, too, when a partner can also empathize with the baby, tell her when she is being unreasonable, and will take the baby and give her a break.

A father, or other partner, needs to be reassured that he is wanted, and that he has valuable goods to offer her and to their growing child. There is room for him. When a father can notice his need for reassurance and love from his partner (and his betrayer, in that she gives so much of her love to their baby), then he may be able to offer her support in the task and tempt her back to their partnership. Then he provides balance and resilience to the Oedipal triangle: one that allows partial exclusion as a fact of life and is counterbalanced by feeling securely, if not exclusively, loved.

For his development, a baby needs his parents to be able to disillusion him gradually, providing him with an additional push to explore outwards and to develop his own resources. The child needs his parents to be reasonably robust: to be able to withstand his challenge and fury without collapse or retaliation – for if not, he is left feeling dangerously powerful. And yet to do so takes considerable emotional strength. It involves the parents being able to accept, painfully, that, in their young child's eyes, they are not only perfect – they are *mean* and *horrible*, too, and that this is necessary and inevitable.

If parents can allow themselves to have their own needs, too, without excessive blame, then it is easier to hold on to sympathy for their child and his distress without feeling overwhelmed by it.

A **2-year-old** waited outside the butcher's shop with her father, and the new baby in the buggy, looking in the window at her mother in the queue. As her wriggling grew, her father brought her in to be with her mother: this settled her for a while but she became restless for her father, now outside. The father came in and held her in his arms. As her mother started to speak to the butcher the little girl screamed – furiously holding out her arms to her mother.

The father commented to the mother how tired and hungry their little girl was.

The little girl had to manage the frustration of being made to wait and having to choose between her mother and father, but she could not have them both. Her mother's paying attention to the butcher was the last straw. In this encounter, the father was able to help the mother and their little girl. Luckily for her, they could sympathize with her and not react with exhausted irritation – which might have left the little girl worried that her frustration and rage had killed off her parents' loving sympathy.

Letting go

> ... *I can see*
> *You walking away from me towards the school*
> *With the pathos of a half-fledged thing set free*
> *Into a wilderness ...*
> *That hesitant figure, eddying away*
> *Like a winged seed loosened from its parent stem ...*
> *selfhood begins with a walking away,*
> *And love is proved in the letting go.*
> (Day Lewis, 2004, 'Walking Away')

While your baby is in your arms you have considerable control, however exhausting. Slowly, the child becomes more independent – and at each stage, while this can be a relief and exciting for the parent, there are also losses.

Once you were the centre of your child's life and, at each step away, each discovery of who and what is interestingly out there, you become less so. You may want your children to get on well without you, to be happy, have resources, friendships – and yet their doing quite so well without you can also be painful. They no longer need you in that same old way.

When the child has ideas of his own this can seem infuriating. To the degree that his parents can bear him to be separate, they can be interested to discover the child they have. When parents are more able to tolerate their child's difference and disagreements without hatred, this helps their child feel that his assertive and aggressive feelings have a place in dealing with the outside world and its demands.

Despite all the other feelings of pleasure, generosity and pride in our child's confidence, there can still be that bit in most of us that can also feel hurt and envious: *how can you do it on your own, without me!* If such resentments are felt as too shameful and are denied, they can be acted out inadvertently by being subtly huffy and wounded at the child's independence or overanxious about risks to them – the source of which can be as much our own unacknowledged hostility.

Parents and their adolescent's sexuality

The physical relationship with a baby or young child can seem relatively straightforward: its intimate carings and the importance and pleasure of touch reassuring to both. When their child reaches an awkward, anxious adolescence, such touch becomes more loaded, more uncertain. Parents are often uneasy about the changing boundary, when suddenly the family contains a pubescent young man or woman, all too aware of their newly sexual body.

In the novel *Lolita*, Nabokov disturbingly presented the sexual pull for the adult when faced with the early adolescent sexuality of the 11-year-old central character. A parent can feel that the only way to keep a safe boundary between him- (or her-) self and the adolescent is by creating a distance. But this can feel to the adolescent as abandonment, as though they are being punished for being somehow bad, without fully knowing why.

Parents can struggle with painful feelings of jealousy and envy at all the exciting new opportunities our children have and hope for.

Just as once we may have resented parents who abandoned us to enjoy their sexual bond, so now we are left out as our child goes off to form new love relationships. Noticing feelings of grief, resentment and envy, as well as of relief and pleasure that our adolescent needs us in a more intermittent way, can be disturbing – but if we can't, we could inadvertently interfere with their pulling away.

> **Karen** had been a single mother. She tried to be a good mother but still she found it hard to bear when her daughter, Fern, was rebellious: she felt that her daughter was ungrateful, after all Karen had given up for her.
>
> She was proud when Fern wanted to stay on at school and had thoughts of further training. But she also worried that Fern would look down on her mother if she did better. Subtly, Karen was mocking and undermining.
>
> It may be no coincidence that Fern got pregnant. Karen felt furious and frustrated at her daughter for falling into the same trap as she had. But she also knew that in one way she would be relieved if Fern gave up plans for her education – for then Fern would not do better than her.
>
> Being able to notice such feelings made Karen miserably guilty, but also concerned for Fern. She told her that she would back her up, whatever she decided to do.

Separating is easier for the adolescent leaving – and hard for the parents who are left behind. It is all too easy to worry. Indeed, young adults can hope to leave worry and sadness all in their parents so that they can feel blithe, free of it themselves: wanting not to notice losses when leaving home and managing on their own.

Part of the job of parenting is to be able to bear being left without turning to hatred or to self-hatred: bearing being important at times, and much less so at others. It is not easy. Some parents respond by being over anxious, some by quickly turning away and refusing to notice ways in which they are still needed.

It might be that wanting to avoid the painful recognition of our frustration and envy at ageing is behind the wish to *show youngsters a thing or two* felt by some middle-aged and older men in sending young men and women in their swaggering prime off to war: and where, while the youngsters risk life and limbs, political leaders are photographed, potent, in uniform on a tank or an aircraft carrier.

To the degree that we can, it helps to be able to put ourselves in our young adult's shoes, recognizing their need to venture out and taking pleasure in it: recognizing, too, how we, not so long ago, may have brought a similar combination of infuriating arrogance, anxiety – and vulnerable charm. But it is a loss and a blow: it helps if there is still the pleasure and reassurance of the arms of partners, friends and the outside world for us to turn back towards.

Note

1 See page 75.

Chapter 17

Work and play

The other side of freedom is the ability to find joy in what one does and the ability to adapt creatively to the inevitable

(Kahneman, 1996).

We can give *work* a bad press, as if it is something best done quickly before getting on to other, more satisfying activities, just a source of frustration and demand. But often it is only if you no longer have a job that you can realize what you did not appreciate at the time: how the income earned as a result of your efforts, the companionship, a sense of achievement and of structuring time are all important parts of self-esteem.

Work is about being able to commit to an activity and having it matter.

Oedipus and work

Oedipal rivalries can be freshly stirred up in the workplace.

Working, whether alone or in a team, stirs up many of the familiar issues already encountered early on: issues of rivalry, envy and jealousy in relation to parents and to siblings – all these are now stirred up in the work situation and can lead to difficulties in learning and in work.

To work well we need to be able to learn from others and value what they have to offer. But this can stir up envy and, if it is felt strongly, then we can denigrate what is on offer and feel rather superior. Being in the position of not knowing everything can feel like a humiliating come-down but if we cannot accept that, it gets in the way of noticing what we do not yet know: what may be a new and interesting way of looking at things. It is hard then to enjoyably learn from others and use their help.

We might be good at supporting others, if they are safely *small* compared to us. But were they to be in any way *better*, then painful feelings of rivalry and envy can get in the way. Work then becomes more pressured and more isolating.

To the degree that we resent those who have value or power, it can be hard to take any authority, since to do so might stir up others' challenge, envy and hatred in turn. It is tempting then to stay safely in the middle, but it can be frustrating if we want to feel free to express ourselves and put our mark on the task in hand – and in that sense to feel fully adult.

> Before being promoted to a managerial post in the NHS, **Ian** had been safely in the middle with the others, criticizing and feeling rather superior to the bosses. In his new position he felt as if he had become like his father – whom he had always despised and undermined.
>
> Ian could see the real need and that his job was to provide as much help as efficiently as possible, but he dreaded that he would be seen as mean if he challenged others. He anxiously avoided doing so, until he was furious – and then he couldn't look his former colleagues in the eye and his voice became harsh. He felt increasingly stressed and isolated.

If Ian could reconsider his resentments of his own father, he might feel freer to take authority and feel that this could be helpful, not harsh.

Having a mind of your own

> *People ... go through their lives ... without ever realising that they are probably thinking other people's thoughts, living by other people's standards, wearing practically what one may call other people's second-hand clothes, and never being themselves for a single moment*
> (Wilde, 1891).

We all face pressure to conform and fit in. Some of the pressure may come from outside: the expectations of parents, teachers and others. But there is also an anxiety coming from within that needs to be addressed, too.

If the only way to feel safe is to please others, then it is risky knowing our own mind, let alone revealing or fighting for what we think or believe. To the degree that we fear that internal parents may be damaged by our aggression, resentment and rivalry, and fear punishment, then we remain inhibited. If we have taken over what is good and envied from another, then there is the risk that anything we have might be snatched and spoiled in turn.

> **David**'s father was a self-made man: ruthless, successful in business and competitive with his first-born son.
>
> As an adolescent and a young adult David was too intimidated to challenge his father directly, but he made up for this by quietly believing himself intellectually one-up. In academia, he rose up the ladder with a particular glee in proving his elders wrong.
>
> But when he wanted to move outside his safe academic niche and write more for the general public, David was in a panic: he felt that he

would be rubbished by his peers, just as he had so successfully rubbished them in the past.

Because of his unacknowledged attack on his father (and father-substitutes), David had no sense of a father who was loved and admired, despite his faults, and envied for his considerable successes: one who might be pleased in his son's success, were he to feel less constantly diminished by him.

Access to these feelings towards an admired, if imperfect, father might offer David internal support in taking the risk of standing up for what he believes in and withstanding rivals' possible challenges.

Having a mind of your own does not mean getting rid of parents and claiming to have invented the wheel, but being able to take from them and others, knowing where it comes from and where it can feel an important part of a firmer base. Having your own different thoughts and feelings are then no longer so dangerously about being one-up and triumphing, but a subject for a sometimes passionate debate.

It becomes more possible to value others and the company and help they offer. *Success* then is more in terms of contact and discussion; hearing and being heard; finding sources of valued help and encouragement – rather than entrenched competition and one-upmanship. Then it can feel safer to be interested in the work for its own sake and to fight for what matters.

Creativity/serious play

When Freud spoke of the capacity to work, he was not just talking about the capacity to hold down a job, but about being free to strive for what you believe in.

Work includes allowing something in life to really matter, the worth of which is not about pleasing anyone else and may be separate from financial gain: taking the risk of really trying and risking that the result will not be as perfect as you might wish.

A child who is playing is not light-hearted: he is often deadly serious, completely absorbed, whether he is playing at a tea party on top of the garden shed or running away from home, to the end of the garden. He is seriously playing with ideas and scenarios: making sense of, and having an impact on, his world.

As adults we often lose this intense, focused idea of play, where the end result may be less the point of the activity but one of curiosity: trying something out and seeing what happens. Winnicott described the child's playing with the necessary presence of his mother in the background, keeping things safe, available, yet not intruding (Winnicott, 1958). As adults too, if we are less busy denigrating or placating parents, then we are more likely to benefit from a sense of a helpful figure internally to help sustain us against disappointments:

Pat was writing a book about his professional work. He worried that his colleagues would be contemptuous if he were less than perfect, or envious if he did well. He knew that if he kept these alarming figures in mind he would produce work that was timid and not really his own. He was not sure how much these figures really existed externally, or were more within his own mind – but pushing them away as much as he could, he felt freer to just muck about and play with his ideas. Even so, each draft he produced was miserably short of what he thought he might have it in him to write. Reality was very painful.

For a while Pat just gave up and turned to other things, but then he would go back to look at what he had written, cut out big chunks of it, keeping only a few sentences or phrases from what he had written earlier. Seeing that some bits were good was cheering – though in a harsh superego part of his mind he thought that a proper writer would be able to do it so much more easily, and therefore, compared to them, he was 'pathetic' and 'wasting his time'.

Pat kept on going in bits, not because he knew any longer whether what he would produce would be a book, but because he was interested in the ideas he slowly pulled out of his mind, like buried relics out of a sludgy river. It was frustrating, exhausting – but deeply satisfying, serious play.

Resilience

You could say that Pat in the above example was being resilient, which he was, but it wasn't to do with being tough and pushing himself on.

It was more to do with a gentleness: reassuring himself, despite all those sneering internal voices, that his attempts were interesting to him, and therefore worthwhile. And that if a book did not emerge out of this serious play, it would be very disappointing, but it would not be a complete disaster. It would not mean that he was worthless.

These gentle, reassuring internal figures were important in Pat's capacity to be resilient – as was feedback from trusted external figures.

Pat had a woman friend whom he would entrust to read his drafts. When she told him that there were good things in what he was doing, but that there were also particular flaws, he hated to hear it, and her for saying it. He respected her for telling him and knew it would have been easier for her to reassure him that everything was *great*.

Often, after his disappointment, hurt and anger with her less than over-whelming response, he needed time to recognize that she was right more often than she was wrong. But still she was wrong sometimes, he thought. Then he could start writing again, chastened – but with some renewed cheer. His view of his friend as essentially helpful had withstood the assault of his anger and he (and she) had survived in the face of her feedback. He felt relieved and grateful.

Holding on to enthusiasm

Success in life consists of going from one failure to another without losing enthusiasm (Abraham Lincoln)

There is a narcissistic part of all of us that wishes that we should get complete success without effort, as of right, a mark of our specialness, and we have to bear the reality of inevitable disappointment and doubt.

Learning anything worthwhile, whether in playing an instrument or honing football skills, takes effort, persistence and a capacity to hold on to some sense of worth in the face of despair. We all need a self-checking mechanism; to bear to see ourselves at moments through someone else's cool eyes – not overly critical, but not overly sympathetic either.

Then we might find that we need to do more groundwork on an idea; take time, think again, let time pass. And then try again.

> In the 1930s, the novelist **John Steinbeck** struggled to write a story of the vast number of people moved off the land as a result of mechanisation, big business and drought, but he could not find the right form. He tried writing in short stories. He completed a version as satire – but he was not satisfied and he wrote to his agent and his publisher: 'This book is finished and it is a bad book and I must get rid of it ... My father would call this a smart-alec book ... If I can't do better I have slipped badly' (Steinbeck & Walsten, 2001).
>
> Steinbeck had a critical, but possibly accurate, internal father. Should he just have accepted less than perfect reality or try again? He could not know.
>
> As he tried writing again in March 1938, Steinbeck wrote to his agent, 'I don't seem to know any more about writing a novel than I did ten years ago. You'd think I would learn. I suppose I could dash it off but I want this one to be pretty good' (Letter to Otis, 23/3/1938).
>
> In the middle of these doubts, these failed efforts, Steinbeck finally found his way. He started writing hard in May 1938. Five months later the manuscript of *Grapes of Wrath* was handed over to the publisher.

It is helpful to be reminded that even the most gifted suffer necessary and sometimes accurate doubt. Failing is part of the scenery. The wish to discover more, try more, is not just neurotic. Accepting reality does not mean being resigned to what you do not have. Some sort of determination to fight for what you want is vital and to keep going in the face of scepticism and doubt: your own as much others'.

Young architect **Basil Spence** told a fellow soldier on the Normandy beaches that if he got out of the war alive, his ambition was to design a cathedral.

After the war, the design for Coventry Cathedral was put out to open competition and 600 architects applied. Spence *did not have the faintest hope of success* (Spence, 1963, p. 24). And yet, despite this and being heavily committed in other work, he went all out to find a design that really pleased him. He wrote:

> *I found solace and contentment working quietly on the design between 9 o'clock in the evening and into the early morning ... I found myself absolutely alone and there were few people who I could talk to who understood or could help. The desert, however, has its attractions and I got to know the Brandenburg Concertos by heart as I played them over and over again while I worked late into the night ...*
>
> (Spence, 1963, p. 30).

His work was solitary, but it was heavily dependent on the support of two others: his wife and friend. Spence won the commission: he then found that there were inevitable new anxieties and obstacles to face. He described

> *'the awful feeling that the finger had pointed at me and I was not worthy or able'*
>
> (Spence, 1963, p. 38).

Enthusiasm, however invaluable, doesn't guarantee us everything. We have to painfully face up to limitations without giving up too soon. Being able to bear such knocks to our narcissism, without turning to hatred and mockery (making what is lost no good, or ourselves useless), only then does it become safer to commit, to risk hopeful effort.

Recognizing feelings and fears, childish and illogical as they might be, does not make them go away. We need all the adult logical, problem-solving techniques that can be mustered – as well as being able to find fond and firm parenting within, to contain and calm our easily panicked self.

Rest

> *Even the so-called chores I turn to joy; the sweeping of a floor, dust slanting in rays of light, the quality of wood or stone, the cleaning of a window, that thrilling insubstantial substance glass, hard against driven rain, yet liquid to light*
>
> (Ede, 2008, p. 10).[1]

Work has such a powerful function, keeping us busy, stopping us noticing what goes on around us and in us, protecting against disturbance or anxiety.

But in fact we need to be able to pause, to take time alone, pay attention rather than just fill time. Jim Ede may have been sweeping the floor, but he also had his senses alert to all that was around him and he was open to the joy in that.

Play: tamed and untamed

For me, excess was a desperate attempt to preserve something inhuman, to hang on to wildness. I knew that being a man had something to do with that wildness: wildness *not savagery, but the wildness of birds and animals, the wildness of a hard wind in the grass, the wildness of the sea, the wildness of things that remain untamed . . .*

(Burnside, 2007, p. 234).

I have spoken about serious play, but of course there is necessary play that is just playful: just for the pleasure of it. Of being, even for a while, less *tamed*. When you play you let go of some of the restraints and demands of your rational mind. You let your hair down. Go for it. It can be wonderful.

As a part of its appeal, it can also have a dangerous, transgressive edge, where having a break, having fun is at the cost of anything or anyone seriously mattering – including yourself. It is possible to gang up against that more vulnerable part of yourself: where drinking, drug-taking, and risk-taking can all be seen as cutting edge. Then you can sneer at a you who is concerned or fearful; who may notice that staying up late drinking or waking up in a stranger's bed is, after a while, not as great as it's cracked up to be.

We still need some sort of internal parental figure keeping us from becoming over-excited, over-aggressive or caught up in a mob where there is a pleasure, but also risks, in handing over responsibility.

When mocking savagery within is less, when being seen as foolish is not the worst thing, then it is safer to take a risk rather than take the piss. Then you can enjoy participating in a sport, playing a musical instrument, singing, dancing, enjoying sex – not as a performance task, having to get it right, but for the fun of it, for the pleasure of feeling alive.

> **Mike** hadn't played guitar since his college days, when he'd played in a band. Very many years later, he picked it up again, strummed a bit and got fed up. Picked it up again and strummed a bit more. Had some lessons. Played a bit with a friend. They thought they might play in an open-mike session in a local pub. It started to feel quietly, deeply satisfying.
>
> He knew that if he put time into it, he would get better – even though sadly, and however much he wished, he would never get to be Eric Clapton.

Note

1 H.S. (Jim) Ede was director of the Tate Gallery and founder of Kettles Yard, Cambridge.

Chapter 18

Mid-life

At the mid-point of the path through life, I found
Myself lost in a wood so dark, the way
Ahead was blotted out. The keening sound
I still make shows how hard it is to say
How harsh and bitter that place felt to me...

(I) can't say even now how I had come
To be there, stunned and following my nose
Away from the straight path.

(Dante, 2013)

In mid-life, those years between the late 40s and the late 60s, the landscape changes in a slow but ground-breaking way. Some of the time you may cheer yourself that you have a lived wisdom. You may be freer. You may be fit, healthy, pleased with life. Your income greater. You may have twenty, thirty good years ahead.

But not since adolescence are you likely to have faced such physical and emotional change. Unlike earlier, time no longer spreads out endlessly before you – and old age is somewhere over the next hill.

Your body is less resilient: aches and pains are felt more routinely; hearing, sight and memory are less acute; energy, including sexual energy, is less reliable. Physically you can fight to smooth out the years' toll with surgery and extreme fitness. But what of the *self* you feel yourself to be? In this middle stage of life, what can feel deeply questioned is a sense of having value to yourself – let alone to anyone else. Relationships with parents, partner, growing children, work, all need to be renegotiated.

In that earlier phase of adulthood there were many stresses and demands, but they were new and challenging: new houses to fix up, new children, new work, new settings. As these became more familiar, so those demands can seem to have taken all your energies, leaving little left that feels quite for *you*. And there are likely to have been costs: your focus narrowed and other areas of curiosity and interest let go.

As well as real external changes to face, there are internal ones too. Under the pressures of mid-life, all those familiar conflicts are freshly stirred up: between loving, appreciative feelings and ones that stem from frustration, envy and jealousy. Earlier on, we may have eased the disappointment of not having everything now by telling ourselves that *sometime* we will. And in mid-life we find that we won't ever have it all. This can still feel a blow. Strategies to protect against feelings of vulnerability, dependence and fear of loss can be bleakly isolating. In an age where youth is so very prized we are no longer young.

As in Dante's description above, this place can be stunning, hard and bitter – and there are many temptations to manage the path in an *un-straight* way.

The loss of being young

A woman's loss of fertility may be a relief, but it is also evidence of ageing. Other, young women may have babies – and no longer she. Wolf-whistles in the street, once so annoying, will not be for her. Women have to renegotiate their sense of their womanliness and their worth. Men might not have such a clear-cut end to their fertility, but they lose their hair, have concerns about the reliability of their potency and may rely more on chemical aids.

Our achievements are finite. Our time may be enough but it is not endless, and presents the problem of how to use the time we have for the best.

Fears of fading physical charm can seem to be all do with external reality. But a sense of beauty and of worth comes from inside as much as out. Those who in the past identified with the young Snow White threatened by the *wicked* older woman (or Peter Pan outwitting Hook), in mid-life may recognize the pain of one who so wants magic reassurance that she is still the *fairest of them all* – and feels murderous when she (or he) is not. Such feelings, which seem so disturbingly ugly, can affect our sense of beauty and worth internally.

When we cannot acknowledge and mourn loss, it can emerge in various less direct ways. Rage can seem to come out of a bright blue sky.

> In Shakespeare's late play, *The Winter's Tale*, **Leontes** seems to be in a happy mid-life: he is married, with a young son and a second on the way.
> But everything is somehow not right. His childhood friend, Polixenes, has been staying for nine months and needs to get back to his own kingdom and his child. But Leontes can't accept that his friend needs to get back to his own life: instead he accuses him of not loving him enough.

Leontes' loss is of his childhood friend: Polixenes has a life of his own elsewhere and Leontes is outside of that. There is also the loss of his wife, Hermione, as his passionate romantic partner to one who has become more known and companionable, and her love affair with their son and the coming baby. His parents have died. Consciously, Leontes seems unaware of these blows.

> He asks his wife to persuade his friend to stay. When she succeeds, Leontes is in a sudden rage: his wife has succeeded where he could not.
>
> He makes sense of his feelings of loss, hurt, jealousy, anxiety and rage by an assumption that his wife and friend are having an affair. He orders his friend to be killed, his new-born baby sent away and he believes his wife dead. He feels justified.
>
> Only when his 9-year-old son dies of distress does reality finally hit home. Leontes spends the next sixteen years in depressive, guilt-struck mourning.

We may be fortunate that we do not have the royal power to do quite the damage that Leontes does, but even so rage and emotional pain, unacknowledged, can be spoiling for others and for ourselves.

Relationship with parents

When parents are still alive, the idea of them still offers us some sort of role as the *younger one*, having some special claim to their concern and care. When they remain healthy there is a buffer between ourselves and our old age and death. As they become more frail that balance shifts: they are able to offer less, and they need us more.

We can feel angry with parents for getting old – and also for leaving us. Being impatient, subtly denigrating, can be a way of expressing grievances from the past as well as in the present. It can also be an attempt to protect against the pain of sadness and loss, for if a parent is just a burden, then the hope is that their death will be just a relief. Resentment and distancing might be an attempt to protect against pain of their eventual loss, but can be a source of regret, too, for it means the loss of closeness in those later years:

> **Chris** had never quite forgiven his father, who had been so busy attending his fragile mother and had such a close bond with her that Chris had been neglected. In his father's later years, Chris had little contact with him, wanting to believe that his father did not matter to him.
>
> In his analysis, he began to retrieve some warmer memories and this was very helpful to him, but it also made him painfully aware that he had squandered what might not have been perfect, but available. Then it seemed better to push those warmer thoughts out of mind once more. It was a miserable dilemma.

A parent's death, whether sudden, or slow and drawn out, can come as more of a loss than you might have expected: often, only then do you realize quite how important was their presence and their relation to that younger you – and how taken for granted.

Re-evaluating a partnership

By mid-life a long partnership can feel overly familiar, with many complaints stored up on both sides – and it can be painful that a long-term partner can recognize your worst points, as well as your best. Seeing your partner's face and body aging can be a troubling reminder of their move towards old-age – and yours, too.

When late adolescent children become more independent and leave home, this may be felt as a relief, but there might also be a painful loss of their company, their liveliness and their central need for you. They are the ones leaving the old and the familiar; you are the one remaining behind. Such situations can stir up wishes to leave home oneself, hoping to leave behind anything *old* and depressing and turn to something or someone fresh.

> **Kev** was in his mid-50s with three boys, all teenage, the eldest about to leave home. He loved being their Dad, the masculine chumminess and banter. He enjoyed feeling like one of the boys, adolescent, ganging up a bit against his wife, Lou.
>
> He minded that Lou had her own closeness to the boys, which made him feel unaccountably left out and wanting to punish her. Sometimes, when he and Lou were close, it was alarming, and it was a relief to get back to the familiar, subtly provocative relationship, which made him feel more of a 'bloke'.
>
> Kev's elder boys were now stronger than him and his youngest boy loved it if he beat him in chess. His eldest brought girls home, and though they were friendly and even a bit flirty, he could see that they were physically drawn to his son, not to him – and that was wounding. He worried about his boys moving on, leaving him behind.
>
> He wanted to show Lou and show his boys that he wasn't just a boring old fart, and found himself having more and more thoughts of starting an affair. He found that idea terrifying – but was that even more of a reason to do it? To show he wasn't just old and scared?

It is hard to know what to do for the best when under this turbulent sway of mid-life: hard to know which of the difficulties are in your partner, your partnership – and which are in you. Whatever the possible gains provided by a new partner, these still do not stop the passage of time. Some whose marriages foundered under such pressure (after feelings of distress, grief, guilt and loss) felt pleased that they had made the break; others found, only later, that they had lost more than they recognized at the time (Wallerstein et al., 2002).

And since, inevitably, in life there is never one right answer, we face regrets whatever our decisions. It can be very painful:

> For Martin Amis, it isn't his work on which his mind lingers. *'It's to do with your children and, more fascinating, how it went with women. That's the big question*

*... women – mistakes, admissions, something that you didn't take far enough –
that all becomes weirdly omnipresent. It turns out to be the most important thing'*
(Cooke, 2006).

Analyst Elliot Jaques considered the types of creativity shown by artists before mid-life, and after (Jaques, 1965).

For many, their earlier work was characterized by an outburst of passionate, driven creativity, spontaneous, *hot from the fire*. Some burned out after this early adult creativity; many (such as Mozart, Keats, Shelley, Rimbaud and Modigliani) died young.

Other creative figures also experienced an emotional crisis in mid-life. They had to face a painful loss of omnipotence and the limits to their dreams of their perfect productions, and to face the ending of life. To the degree that they could face this depressive crisis, they could begin to be creative once more but in a more reflective way. After their return to creative work, the mood changed and became deeper and richer. Michelangelo, Goethe and Shakespeare all showed this change in their work. Their work became more *sculpted*, not only the result of an impetuous outpouring, but one which was honed through thoughtful struggle.

These artists' struggle is ours, too, in hoping to find a way through the emotional strains of this phase of life in ways that allow us to remain open to what life has to offer. Mature creativity includes the capacity to commit, knowing that the end result won't be perfect, and the capacity to be loving – though separateness and difference still stings. If those can be tolerated, we are freer to be creative and open in mid-life and on. Activity then can be out of the love for it, wanting to make something of the activity rather than being fuelled by something more driven. There are limits, necessarily, to our dreams and aspirations: if we cannot bear to see these, then we have to keep on pushing or resentfully finding someone to blame.

When striving and risking disappointment may be no less hard in mid-life than they ever were, age can be a good excuse for giving up wanting anything. *Too late now!* can look as if it might be mature resignation – but might be more to do with wanting to stay in a risk-free comfort-zone.

To rage or not to rage?

Dylan Thomas famously admonished his ageing father,

Do not go gentle into that good night ...
Rage, rage against the dying of the light.
(Thomas, 2014)

Rage may sound enlivening. It can act as a counterweight to misery, resignation and loss of hope. Rage has a point if it's about a capacity to remain passionate about anything, or anyone – not just giving up.

At the same time, it may use up energy in furiously wishing to *make it so*: as if only you stamp up and down enough, then extra of everything – health, years, success, love – will fall into your lap. Just raging at the reality of becoming old, your body and mind less robust, carries the risk of staying aggrieved and stuck.

> **Jim** felt boyishly pleased to reject all the others who were concerned at his hectic life-style and his enthusiastic skiing: much of the pleasure was in proving to them and to himself that he wasn't *past it*.
>
> Until he suffered a bad fall and a nasty fracture. The blow was not only physical but emotional – to his sense of himself as being able to beat age. And then he became very depressed.

Like a climber at a rock face, rage at aging can be counterproductive. It may be more useful to look carefully for foot- and hand-holds, a possible path upwards, a preparedness to compromise if necessary – and to provide protection for if, or when, we fall.

There may be a particular cultural attitude to ageing, but there is an internal source, too. A part of dismay at ageing, at seeing a face in the mirror with disturbing echoes of your father or mother at the time when you were leaving home and at your most superiorly adolescent – is that suddenly you find those superior eyes are turned on you.

Finding yourself in those once-scorned middle-aged shoes, there may be a point in reconsidering whether parents were quite as useless as you had assumed. Did we denigrate those older ones as a way of claiming everything for ourselves out of anxiety – and out of envy?

With the vantage point of age and maybe parenthood, there may be more to sympathize with in our own parents: when they were at the end of their tether, had their own anxieties, insecurities and depressions, their conflict between wishing to attend to their own needs as well as those of us, their children. What they did offer, and their assets and abilities, may be noticed more, too. They might not have been perfect, but not necessarily quite as rubbish as we had painted them.

Noticing this is not always easy. It faces us with depressive anxieties: shame and grief at what we did not appreciate and we missed out on, the loss of the narcissistic self-belief that so much was ours and now seems less than we believed, and more aware of shameful feelings of our envy and hate as well as loving ones.

However, when parents and others, previously taken for granted, are mourned and missed, then our sense of parents internally may soften. It offers the possibility to recognize the value of others more, in the present.

Mid-life is the last phase of seriously productive/energetic life – and brings with it questions of *how do you want to spend your time?* and *with whom?*

> **Paul** took early retirement from his demanding NHS job and he and his wife moved to a smallholding in Wales, with pigs, a holiday cottage

and friends who came to stay, see them, and walk in the glorious countryside. Five years on they still love it. There may come a time when they will have to give up the smallholding or want to move closer to town.

But for the time being they feel they are having a very lively, interesting chapter to their lives and are pleased to have grabbed the opportunity.

Mid-life can be a good moment to finally prioritize yourself. Some use extra time or money to travel and have interesting experiences. Others choose to look inward, not for a quick fix but to really know themselves more, hoping to feel freer to live the remainder of their lives for the best.

Though her life looked more or less all right, in her mid 50s **Sonia** felt life was an effort: she felt a bit martyred, a bit frenzied in a way she did not like. She could cope, but wondered whether analytic help might help her feel less bleak. If she cut down on a lot of other things she could afford it; this was her last chance and she had better make it matter.

She expected her analyst to be sympathetic to her and she was some of the time, noticing how Sonia could quickly drift away, assuming that there was little on offer – like a baby with a mother who is depressed. At other times, her analyst pointed out how she seemed to do this when she felt her analyst had something valued – and that was painful to notice, though she could begin to see how it might make sense.

Opening this all up to scrutiny made Sonia feel uncomfortably flawed and all too human: she could recognize painful feelings of envy and deprivation when someone had more than she. She did too much for others, partly to forestall feelings of guilt – but then felt hard done by and resentful, which started the cycle once more. It was also a quiet self-punishment for what she somewhere also knew: how she quietly punished others to make up for deprivations from early on.

But facing these uncomfortable feelings also made her feel more alive and engaged with herself, and with others, too.

In facing and mourning the sting of disappointments, there are also considerable freedoms and opportunities. Though not endless, there is still time – with luck and our own efforts.

Physically, health may have its own agenda, but even so we have some control through how much we exercise, eat and drink. Emotionally, too, we have some control of the degree to which we let others matter, and things matter, which makes life a richer, fuller experience, if also potentially more risky and painful.

Mid-life is a time to re-find enthusiasm based not on denial, but on valuing what life still has to offer, using the time and energy we have for the best, however long that good time might last. Mid-life offers us the chance to make changes, learning what we can from our experiences and our failures. Activity can be out of the love for it rather than being fuelled by something more driven and sullen: wanting to be the best – and crushing yourself when you are not.

There is no guarantee how long this reasonably healthy, energetic phase will last – maybe a few years, for some lucky people it will be many years. It can only be used for the time being: potent, though not omnipotent.

Chapter 19

Old age

We displayed an unmistakable tendency to 'shelve' death, to eliminate it from life. We tried to hush it up. ... That is our own death, of course. ... No-one believes in his own death. ... In the unconscious everyone is convinced of his own immortality

(Freud, 1915b, p. 91).

In older age, the landscape inescapably alters: threats to physical health, to mental integrity, and emotional strain appear more than ever before. In an age where medical intervention has prolonged our healthy lives, but still faces us with similar lengths of unwell life, many fear a lingering dying beyond when we are physically or mentally competent. And some are fighting for further control of our own dying.

It is also possible to become so anxiously preoccupied with those threats that they inhibit us from just getting on with living as best we can, while we can.

Retirement

And now I have a dog called Elderly
And all he ever wants to do
Is now and then be let out for a piss
But spend the rest of his lifetime sleeping on my lap in front of the fire
(Adrian Mitchell, 1996)[1]

Retirement may be a long-awaited relief but it also offers anxieties and losses, with lessening of income and loss of contact with others in an everyday, but reassuring, way. It can also mean a loss of role, of knowing who you are and that you have value, which is a painful loss at whatever stage of life.

One very active, **former captain of industry** commented how, post-retirement, now old, no one looks at him.

Continuing to work might be tempting, out of ongoing pleasure in the activity and needing to keep earning – but it could also be as much to do with protecting yourself against the loss and anxieties retirement brings. Delaying retirement might look as if it will push back death – but sometimes it just shortens a period of less pressured time.

> **Mary**'s husband John became ill and died, unexpectedly at 67. She suddenly felt angry that they had not both retired earlier, and then been able to have more shared good time together. She had assumed they would live well into their 80s, they both had seemed so fit. Only now, looking back, did she realize how that belief had protected her from the pain of worry, but may have also not allowed her to properly attend to reality.

There is no guarantee how long this reasonably healthy, energetic phase will last: a few years or, for some lucky ones, many. It can only be used for the time being.

Money, or limits on it, make activities harder. But it is not money alone that puts limits on new activities: some go camping in large, comfortable tents; others swap houses with people around the world; some take a degree; some find new challenges and passions; others still find pleasure and contentment in looking after grandchildren.

The problem then may be less to do with literal poverty, but with a sense of internal emotional resources or their lack.

Fear of dependence

Wanting to remain independent can be an anxious worry for people as they get older, fearing the indignities dependence may bring. But too much independence has its own costs, and acknowledging some dependence and need can be nurturing and enabling.

> In the early years of her retirement and after a full working life, **Kay** happily settled into her new village, close by old friends. She had friends, interests and acquaintances. But as the years passed, and with increasing physical disabilities, she decided to arrange for a carer to live in.
>
> At the beginning anyway, she could have coped if she had to – but she liked having her meals cooked for her; she was fond of her younger carer and she felt less anxious with someone in the house at nights.
>
> In that sense, Kay was caring for herself, the *her* who felt more vulnerable with increasing age, in allowing and providing for someone to care for her, and it was better for her to organize it for herself when she could than wait till she was overwhelmed and then might have had to go into a care home.

Illness

One who suffers serious illness may face physical pain, intrusive interventions and indignities.

Emotionally too, illness stirs up primitive feelings of being dependent, fearful and angry. Illness can feel unfair and you can resent those who do not suffer as you do. It can feel like a punishment for your faults. What can make it worse is when you feel that you should not feel fearful, angry and dependent and just be heroic, cheerful and long-suffering. But if so, it may mean that you can't let others close, and you are more isolated at a time when you need comfort most.

Those whose loved one is seriously ill may feel similarly that there is no space to be frightened, fearful and angry *for* their loved one – and *with* them, for getting ill in this way. If we are too fearful of serious illness in a loved partner, family member or friend, then we will turn away and be less engaged emotionally, taking practical care but protecting against getting too emotionally close, for fear that the future loss of them will be too hard to bear. But the more we pull back, the more we isolate ourselves and miss out on what is available in the present.

Death of a loved one

The death of a loved one, particularly after the stress of a long-drawn-out illness, can be a relief as well as a painful loss, and this can be confusing.

There is sadness for the one whose life has been cut short – and for yourself, left lonely by them. There is not only sadness but anger, too; feelings of anger towards the one who has abandoned you, for all that they (and you) did or did not do and now never will. Guilt can then get in the way of painful grief and, in time, allowing yourself a life which has renewed meaning and pleasure.

It is easier to acknowledge feelings of resentment when the relationship has been largely good and when loving feelings mitigate the hostile ones. When this is not so, paradoxically it can be particularly painful to do. Avoiding feelings of resentment at a partner out of guilt can keep people stuck in chronic mourning (Murray Parkes, 1986).

Rage

It is useful not to become too sentimental about ageing, nor expect only serenity from someone suffering the indignities of old age. In 'The Spur', W. B. Yeats (2000) put it vividly:

> *You think it horrible that lust and rage*
> *Should dance attendance upon my old age;*
> *They were not such a plague when I was young;*
> *What else do I have to spur me into song?*

Balance

It can be possible to be overly careful of oneself in old age. Some things may still be worth doing even though they are exhausting – and having to recover from moments of over-exertion is not necessarily the worst thing in the world.

> **Peter**, at 88, agreed, rather anxiously, to go on a weekend trip with his daughter and his teenage grandson, involving a long drive, visiting a famous garden, a medieval town and some beautiful stained-glass windows. He was relieved to be back home, but he had good memories, including the sights, the companionship and the conversations, for his storehouse of memories to warm him over the coming months.

Savouring the small things, in the moment, is something that may be easier to notice in older age than in earlier times, when there was so much else to do. Life can still feel a blessing, despite limitations.

> Peter, though increasingly frail gained much pleasure from watching the birds in his garden.

Knowing that time is limited, can make pleasures in the moment even more appreciated.

> **Paula** had terminal cancer. Her pain was not intolerable though it was now chronic – and she worried about the worse to come. Sometimes she wondered whether it wouldn't be a relief to catch an infection, which would get her suffering over with.
>
> But she was also aware of the great pleasure she still had in life from moment to moment that made life still worth living and, before her illness, this would have surprised her.

Memories

Getting older offers a wider and a longer perspective. Experience and time offers the opportunity to see your life and that of others' developing over time. Long histories unfold: marriages happen, have difficulties and some survive while others don't; children grow, have their difficulties and distresses and their joys and successes; they have families in their turn; parents and others die – some much too early and others after a painfully lingering death.

We notice how old our dear friends (as well as the face in the mirror) have become, before they smile, their eyes light up, and with luck we re-find a still lively *them*, however battered at the edges. These companions from various stages of life are part of the patchwork of our lives, and offer a sense of continuity and comradeship. And the loss of those we love is of those who share those precious memories.

Remembering the past will involve regrets – at what you did and what you did not do – and sadness at what and who has been lost. Only if you can allow yourself to wander through past experiences do you also stand to reap the ongoing pleasure from them. For memories are a storehouse from an experience of a good-enough life.

We feel more accompanied, more connected: we have imperfect but loved and loving figures internally. It is easier then to reach out and engage with the outside world when we find ourselves less deprived, less resentful and more able to tolerate feelings that include envy. Then we are more able to enjoy others, be interested in them and their discoveries and want to help and support them.

Paradoxically, if death can be looked in the eye, then it may make it easier to live life as fully as possible until the end. A 95-year-old blogger wrote of her upcoming visit to Brazil:

> *If I die when I am there, then they can incinerate me and send me home in a little box. I'll be a bit bruised by the time I get there, but this is an opportunity I won't have again*
>
> (Lopez, 2007).

While most of us won't have Maria Amelia Lopez's insouciance, let alone her energy, there is still that sense in which things may be worth doing even if we will not see them to fruition.

Literary editor, then writer, Diana Athill wrote powerfully about her life at 89 (Athill, 2008). Early in her book she described the disappointment of receiving a sapling tree fern with only four frail little leaves – not at all like the big one she had hoped to be able to plant out in her garden. Nevertheless she potted it on. By the end of the writing, some years later, the fern had nine fronds. Athill concludes: '*I was right in thinking I will never see it being a tree, but I underestimated the pleasure of watching it be a fern. It was worth buying*' (Athill, 2008, p. 183).

Note

1   A comparison with his *Puppy called Puberty* on page 92.

Chapter 20

Conclusion

I cannot tell you how often I think of a sentence you spoke to me once ... that it does not matter what fate one has if one only really lives it.
(Anna Freud to Lou Andreas-Salomé, 1932;
Young-Bruehl, 2008, p. 230)

Freud famously described the ability of psychoanalysis to change *hysterical misery into common unhappiness* (Freud, 1893, p. 305) and it can seem as if all he holds out is the promise of something drearily grim and grey.

In fact, what Freud is speaking of is moving from that state of extremes: the addictive, exciting lure of triumph and having it all, even if offset by its alarming downside, being the lowest of the low, humiliated and despised. Loosening the tight grip of this extreme, demanding state means being more able to tolerate reality, imperfect as it is – as we are.

To the extent that we can understand, accept and have some sympathy with ourselves, like an internal parent, fond but firm, then we are more able to withstand the worst of our criticism and self-doubt. We need to find ways to be able to tolerate the sadness of losses, guilt at our less honourable impulses, what we do out of hostility, and what we do not do out of anxiety and shame.

Having some capacity to tolerate disturbing feelings makes it possible to risk more. We need to tolerate feelings of envy if we are to fully value another, or ones of disappointment to risk reaching out. Only if we have some trust in our capacity to survive the pain of loss can we risk really loving, or fully committing to an endeavour, knowing it will never be as good as we may wish.

If failure, being less than perfect, is a painful part of life but really not an intolerable disaster, then we are freer to notice. We need to have time alone and for silence – since this is the only way we will know what is going on within us. We are more able to have room for desire – for something or someone, rather than needing to keep a gap filled. Then we can engage in life more fully rather than being caught up in inner anxieties. The world then is not something grey and desiccated, or only extremes of black and white, but becomes more three dimensional, more coloured.

There is no perfect, pain-free alternative to reality. Things go wrong. Stuff happens. We are not the centre of the universe in which others' task is to revolve around us, offering the perfect combination of nurture, freedom and guaranteed success.

Even if you were an only child, with parents happy together, there is still the pain of observing their happiness when some of the time you are on the outside. Were they to have rowed more, it might be less enviably excluding – but more alarming. Having a parent (or parents) who are only adoring can become restricting, making it harder to find what life has to offer outside those safe confines. Being reassured that you are uniquely special makes it tougher to learn to face that sometimes you have to struggle – and even then won't be quite as special as you wish.

Blows are a necessary part of the territory. Like clearing out an old junk-room, if you can sort out what in your mind is well past its sell-by date and time to give up, you have room to notice what still has value in its old rough way.

Excitement, self-belief and hope are a vital part of our determination and liveliness, but such excitement is less frantic when its counterpart is not worthlessness but being flawed, less than perfect, all too human. You end up with more space in mind, more flexibility. You are firmer, more integrated.

These discoveries are often not startlingly new, but frequently something half-known, but never before so emotionally alive. As T. S. Eliot wrote:

And the end of all our exploring
Will be to arrive where we started
And know the place for the first time.

So, finally, I have to allow myself to finish, with always more to say and to say better. I have to allow it out of my anxious grip and send it out into the world trusting (as U. A. Fanthorpe put it) in *luck and the kindness of other people* (1992).

Appendices

In these appendices, I offer summaries of some of Freud's famous case histories (Appendices A–E) and an account of Klein's Richard (Appendix F), all of which give gripping detail that, for reasons of patient confidentiality in the vignettes I have offered, I have not been able to do.

Appendix A

Anna O (Bertha Pappenheim)

Anna O was a bright, unmarried, daughter in an extremely wealthy Jewish family. In the absence of other things to absorb the interest of such a young woman in those stultifying times, she lived much of the time in the 'private theatre' of her imagination. When her father was dying, she attended to him devotedly – rather to the exclusion of her mother and sister. Anna developed a variety of psychosomatic symptoms, which made it impossible for her to care more for him and she was barred from the sickroom.

This determined young woman effectively showed her physician, Josef Breuer, what she needed to alleviate her symptoms: being allowed to 'chimney sweep' – recalling and acknowledging the events and her thoughts which had occurred at the time of the development of a symptom. Conscious recall led to the symptom disappearing. So she told her physician of hearing dance music when waiting at her father's bedside and her wish that she could go: a shameful thought which she had quickly suppressed.

An intense daily bond developed between Anna O and her doctor. She was demanding of Breuer and for a while she refused to eat unless spoon-fed by him. Breuer's wife was jealous and insisted on taking him away on holiday, which resulted in a pregnancy – which Anna would have heard about from mutual connections.

Following this time, Anna O's symptoms increased. She now needed to recall not only the events of the current day but also, day by day, the events of the previous year. At the end of this year of recall, Anna O went into a hysterical labour, 'giving birth' to Breuer's child. It was as if by remaking the previous year in Breuer's presence, Anna had been attempting to undo the fact of his holiday and, in her wishful imagination, making herself the one pregnant instead (Britton, 2005).

Despite this ending, and though she never married, Anna O (Bertha Pappenheim) did well and put her remarkable energies into psychoanalytic social work.

Appendix B

Dora (Ida Bauer): seen 1900 (published 1905)

Eighteen-year-old Dora presented with a nervous cough, other fluctuating physical symptoms and a two-year unbudging dislike of her former confidante, whom she (correctly) believed was her father's mistress, the less well-off Frau K. She had written a suicide note, meaning to frighten her father into giving up his affair. Her father hoped that Freud would resolve Dora's opposition.

Dora's parents were unhappy. She did not get on well with her mother, who was described as an obsessional housewife, with cleaning rituals which Freud thought were in response to receiving a chronic gonorrhoeal infection from her husband. Family friendship seemed a cover for her father's affair.

Four years earlier, Frau K's husband had kissed the then 14-year-old Dora – and she could still remember the pressure of *his chest on her body*. He daily sent her flowers. Following the kiss, Dora had a repetitive dream:

> A house was on fire. My father was standing beside my bed and woke me up. I dressed quickly. Mother wanted to stop and save her jewel-case; but Father said: "I refuse to let myself and my two children be burnt for the sake of your jewel-case." We hurried downstairs, and as soon as I was outside I woke up.

Two years later, on a family holiday, K propositioned Dora, telling her that he *got nothing from his wife* (a form of words Dora knew K had used to a governess, whom he had then abandoned). Dora slapped him. That afternoon, when she was having a nap, he turned up in her bedroom. She subsequently locked the door – but the key was then removed. Dora decided not to remain with the Ks but to return home with her father.

Only after two weeks, with no word from K, did Dora tell her parents of his attempted seduction. When challenged, K first promised to come and sort it all out. But then he changed his mind and claimed that it was all a figment of Dora's imagination. He was backed up in this by Frau K, who said that Dora *always wanted to talk about sex*.

Dora was furious at this treble betrayal – by K, by Frau K, and by her father's refusal to give up Frau K in the light of his daughter's distress.

Freud thought that Dora was more excited, more actively involved in the flirtation than she wanted to let herself admit. He thought that Dora's memory of K's *chest* pressing against her as he kissed her when she was 14 was an upward displacement of her awareness of K's erection. He thought that K's proposition to her was probably exciting as well as disturbing to the 16-year-old, who was keen to learn from Frau K about sex and to read her illuminating sexual books. Freud thought that Dora's fury might be less that K propositioned her in the first place, but that he did not follow up her suit after she had slapped him – leaving her hurt and humiliated.

Freud was not critical of Dora for her sexual interest but thought that, unacknowledged, it contributed to her hysterical physical symptoms. He wondered whether the two men had an agreement: Herr K's wife in exchange for Dora; also about the mutual attraction between the two (as shown in the daily sending and accepting of flowers) and whether marriage might be a possible best outcome.

In relation to Dora's repetitive dream, Freud linked her memory of her father coming to wake her in the night to prevent bed-wetting, and to other wetness from childhood masturbation and sexual excitement linked to her father: Dora said she 'could not remember' this. Freud then brought possible corroboration from a clinical observation:

> a few days later she did something which I could not help regarding as a further step towards the confession. For on that day she wore at her waist— a thing she never did on any other occasion before or after—a small reticule [a drawstring handbag] of a shape which had just come into fashion; and, as she lay on the sofa and talked, she kept playing with it— opening it, putting a finger into it, shutting it again, and so on (p. 76).

Freud pointed out to Dora how she was inadvertently confirming his suspicion of her childhood masturbation.

Two weeks later Dora walked out of treatment.

By walking out, Freud thought that Dora had taken revenge on him – as she had on K and her father. Freud thought that behind Dora's interest in Herr K was her father – whose love she wanted all to herself. And behind that was her love for Frau K. With hindsight, we might wonder, too, whether there isn't a longed-for mother also, denigrated and lost as any sort of helpful, admirable female figure.

We may wonder about the role of Dora's father in encouraging this friendship and of her mother in ignoring the meaning of a daily gift of flowers. But Dora, too, had her part: she wanted to keep seeing herself as only innocent, a victim – but in a way which kept her stuck. Instead, her frustration, fury and confusion were expressed through bodily symptoms such as her nervous cough. As in her dream, Dora had succeeded in protecting her *jewellery box* – her physical chastity – and her sense of aggrieved innocence, but this was at the cost of the house burning down: she had no longer had access to her active wishes and interests.

Some 23 years after the end of this interrupted treatment, Dora, then forty-one consulted the analyst Felix Deutsch in New York. She had married unhappily and had one son. She remained symptomatic: frigid, complaining, bedbound, dizzy and was distraught at her now-adult son's leaving her for other sexual partners (Deutsch, 1957).

Meanwhile her brother, who was much closer to the despised mother, went on to become an admired politician (Deutsch, 1957).

Appendix C

Little Hans: (Herbert Graf) (treated 1908) (Freud, 1909b)

Freud was delighted to have the opportunity of learning more about a young child's phantasies and wishes, through his work with a 5-year-old little boy who had become phobic of going out, for fear that a horse would bite him. He only saw the boy once directly, but instead worked through the boy's father, a colleague of his.

Little Hans seems to have been a delightful, curious 5-year-old, pleased and relieved to talk with his father about his fears, his dreams and his less acceptable feelings towards both parents, without his father being shocked or judgemental.

Little Hans' fear of going out had started after seeing a horse being beaten in the street: he was horrified – but also fascinated. He told his father of his wish to be able to return to a previous summer, when he'd had his mother to himself and his father had visited only at weekends – and before the birth of his baby sister (by this time 18 months old).

Little Hans was very interested in his 'widdler'. He was fascinated by the large size of horses' widdlers, and thought his mother probably had a huge one, too. He enjoyed his penis being touched and touching himself and he seemed unconcerned when his exasperated mother threatened that, if he kept touching it himself, his widdler would be cut off. He saw his baby sister naked and commented on her 'sweet little widdler'.

The boy was very curious to know how his baby sister had arrived – and did not believe his parents' story that the stork had brought her. He had heard his mother groaning in labour and seen blood in a basin and knew that in some alarming way this was linked to the baby's arrival. He believed that his sister had been present the summer before her birth *in a box*: possibly a reference to his mother's swelling belly. Under Freud's direction, the father gave his son some sexual information.

Little Hans was also interested in the idea of having babies himself and linked them with his bodily products, his *lumf* (faeces). He thought that, like his mother, he, too, might receive babies from his father. When his father suggested to him that he might wish that his father would fall down like the horse in the street, or be whipped, so that he could get his mother all to himself, Little Hans agreed with evident relief.

> He told his father of anxious thoughts that a plumber might come: "The plumber came; and first he took away my behind with a pair of pincers, and then gave me another, and then the same with my widdler"
>
> (Freud, 1909b, p. 95).

The little boy worried, too, that if he fell in the bath, his mother would not rescue him – and again agreed with his father's suggestion that he feared his mother would no longer love him if she knew of his angry wishes – including that his baby sister would drown.

The boy happily thought that if his father were to marry *his* mother, then he, Little Hans, could safely marry his mother and they could have lots of babies together.

The young boy's fears receded. As an adult, Little Hans (Herbert Graf) was able to use his energies in a creative way, becoming a successful opera producer/director.

Appendix D

The 'Rat Man': Paul Lorenz (PL) (1907) (Freud, 1909a)

The 29-year-old young man came to Freud for help with tormenting obsessional thoughts that something terrible would happen to his father (who by then had been dead for 8 years) and to a young woman he called 'his lady' - even though she had rejected him for a second time four years previously. He had suffered from obsessional ideas on and off since childhood.

PL's rat obsession had been set off while on recent military service manoeuvres: he had been told by a sadistic army captain of a punishment where a rat was trapped over a prisoner's anus and would gnaw his way out through the prisoner's body. The young man had the horrific, and yet also exciting, thought that this punishment could happen to his father and to 'his lady', unless he did something to forestall it.

The sadistic captain later told PL that he owed a Lieutenant A money, for a pair of replacement glasses which had been sent for. PL knew the money was not really owed to him, for he had already been told that the young woman at the post office had paid the money. Still, he vowed to pay the lieutenant. He knew it was ridiculous, but he could not let go his dread that if he did not carry out his promise, in every way, the terrible punishment might happen.

The story became increasingly convoluted. Should the money go to Lieutenant A – or rather to Lieutenant B? The young man started on the train back home, continuing to agonize how he might, even now, go and get both lieutenants to come with him to the post office, where he could give the money to A, who could give it to the young woman ... etc.

Freud tells us how the young PL had an explosive temper, possibly linked to the intrusions and excitement of early experiences of sexual touching with various nursemaids.

At 3, when beaten by his father for biting, he had gone into a rage and yelled childlike curses at his father, who commented that his little son would become 'either a great man or a criminal'. From that time on he became a coward. (Around the time of his outburst, an elder sister was sick and she died the following year.)

Some years later, he invited his younger brother, of whom he was jealous, to look up the packed barrel of his toy gun, shot him – and was disappointed not to hurt him (Freud, 1909a p. 184).

When the 12-year-old PL felt himself to be in love with a young girl, he had the thought that were his father to die, the girl would feel sympathetic to him. He subsequently became very religious, stopped masturbating and tried to keep everybody safe with prayers – 'may God protect them' – but into which *not*, 'may God not protect ...' invariably crept.

PL described 'the first real blow of [his] life' when, at 15, it became clear that an admiring older boy who became his tutor was really more interested in his elder sister than in him (Freud, 1909a, p. 41).

At 20, the young man began some sort of relationship with 'his lady': it is possible that the relationship was always more in his mind than reality – for his father told him early on that 'he should keep away ... and would only make a fool of himself'. The lady rejected him. His father died – and PL did not mourn (Freud, 1909a, p. 82).

Once, his lady was dismissive of him in public and he was mortified: when he challenged her, she denied (possibly unconvincingly) that she had meant it in such a negative way. For a while PL would obsessionally ask everyone the precise meaning of each phrase they spoke. Not surprisingly, his lady rejected him a second time.

The Rat Man's love for his lady was narcissistic: it was for someone who should be 'his', since he wished it, rather than bear the painful reality that, after two rejections, she really was not. Instead he stayed stuck, refusing to accept reality and torn between his hateful feelings, and his parallel wish to protect her.

A year after his father's death, and after the death of an aunt, PL began to ruminate obsessionally on his father's death. He kept his father alive in a magical way: opening the door to him at night, supposedly to show his father how hard he was studying – but in fact defying him, exposing his genitals and looking at himself in the mirror. When he finally lost his virginity at 26 (and though his father had been dead five years by then) one of his thoughts was 'One might murder one's father for this!' (Freud, 1909a, p. 82).

Hateful, murderous wishes and his horror of them meant that the young man was consumed with anxious guilt – although displaced on to something else (the need to repay the money he did not in fact owe). He told his analyst, with agony, of his hateful feelings for him, too: so when he got Freud's bill, he had the thought: 'so many sessions, so many rats'. He believed Freud's brother was in prison – and laughed at the possibility.

PL associated the rat with sex, infection, syphilis and his penis; with children; with money; in an identification with his father, who as a young soldier had been a *spielratten* (a gambler); with a rat seen running over his father's grave which he thought, might have just feasted off his father's corpse. He connected himself with the rat too – he had been *such a nasty, dirty little wretch apt to bite* ... (Freud, 1909a, p. 216).

The young man was touched by his analyst's understanding and lack of condemnation for his hostile and murderous impulses – but his relief at Freud's sympathy quickly turned to excitement and triumph: his analyst must want him as a son-in-law! He then had a dream of Freud's daughter, someone he had seen on the stairs, with *dung instead of eyes* (Freud, 1909a, p. 200).

Freud's treatment over nine months helped the young man to put his thoughts into words, have them heard without condemnation – and without his hateful wishes leading to disaster. PL was able to let go of his pressing rat obsessions, if probably not the full extent of his underlying disturbance. He was killed some years later, along with so many other young men, in the convulsions of the Great War.

Appendix E

The Wolf Man: Sergei Panchikoff (SP) (1910–1914) (Freud, 1918)

This immensely wealthy and emotionally deprived 23-year-old Russian, came to Freud suffering from symptoms of depression, suspicion and feeling not quite alive. Physically, he needed daily enemas to manage constipation. He dated the onset of his symptoms to an outbreak of gonorrhoea five years previously.

The year prior to coming to Freud, SP's elder sister, Anna, had killed herself, followed some months later by his father. Consciously, the young man experienced no feelings of loss, but instead was pleased that he did not have to share the family wealth with his sister.

When he was growing up, SP's mother suffered from ill health and had little active involvement with her children. His father, a politician, suffered from manic–depressive episodes. In summer, the family moved to their second Estate, and the parents would go off for a few weeks alone. His closest relationship was to a beloved Nanny.

At 3, while his parents were away, his sister Anna, then 10, exposed herself to him and played with his penis. When the young Sergei in turn exposed himself to his Nanny, she warned him that such acts could lead to being left with a 'wound'. The boy felt this as a rejection and he responded by being cruel to animals – and then fearing that they had been hurt. On his parents' return, feeling that his father showed more interest in his precociously talented older sister, the little boy was defiant, provoking his father to punish him.

At 4, and following a dream, the little boy developed a phobia of wolves and would scream at a picture of a wolf standing on its hind legs (which his sister delighted in showing him) and he feared being eaten by one.

When Sergei was 6, his father had a depressive breakdown and spent six months in a sanatorium: the boy was taken to visit and was anxious for his crushed father.

As a teenager, he turned his voracious sexual attention to a young housemaid and others. Freud thought that he chose partners who were beneath him, turning his passive experience of his sister's seduction into an active one, thus revenging himself on his sister.

Freud treated the Wolf Man for over four years, describing him as 'unassailably entrenched behind an attitude of obliging apathy ... when he began for the first time to feel relief, he immediately gave up working in order to avoid any other changes ...' (Freud, 1918, p. 11).

Freud managed his patient's passivity by setting a termination date four months in the future. In that time they worked to unpick SP's childhood dream of wolves that had sparked off his phobia. In his dream at 4 years old:

> *I dreamt that it was night and that I was lying in my bed ... Suddenly the window opened of its own accord, and I was terrified to see that some white wolves were sitting on the big walnut tree in front of the window. There were six or seven of them. The wolves were quite white ... they had big tails like foxes and they had their ears pricked like dogs when they pay attention to something. In great terror, evidently of being eaten up by the wolves, I screamed and woke up*
>
> (Freud, 1918, p. 29).

His adult association was to a childhood story of wolves, where an old (father) wolf is tricked and left tail-less. But there is a threat of punishment – for the wolves might eat him.

With his patient, Freud reconstructed childhood events in the following, arguably unconvincing, way:

> when the boy had been 18 months old, sick and therefore sleeping in his parents' bedroom, he had woken up (*the windows opening*), and seen his parents active in intercourse (the opposite of *very still*): his father entering his mother from behind and from which vantage point the toddler might have seen his father's erect penis appearing and disappearing inside his

mother. This offered the child the alarming evidence of genital differences, and the implication that he (and his penis) really could be attacked by his wolf/father as a result of his hostile wishes towards him.

Only when the little boy's nanny threatened a wound to his penis did the earlier experience (of his mother's lack of a penis) have a sudden, terrifying, retrospective force.

Freud thought that his patient was just as likely to have gained evidence of sexual difference from watching sheep rutting on the family estate and he was only persuaded of it by his patient's enthusiasm for the more exciting version – which SP later rebutted.

But the reconstruction does not affect Freud's main analytic point: that an earlier sight of no penis suddenly makes a threat to his own penis dreadfully possible. The interpretative work done as a result of this dream helped the young man finish his studies; he returned to Russia where he set up a law practice and married.

During the Russian Revolution, SP lost all his lands. He returned to Vienna, gaining considerable attention as Freud's famous patient, the Wolf Man. By that time Freud had been operated on for oral cancer, was looking frail and had a prosthesis in his jaw. Freud arranged a collection to help the impoverished SP for six years.

The Wolf Man had renewed symptoms – of constipation and a delusional belief that he had a hole in his nose. He went into treatment with another analyst, who took up his excited hostile feelings towards Freud. (Mack Brunswick, 1928). So SP said of an ill doctor, whom he associated with Freud: '*how agreeable it is that I, the patient, am really healthy, whereas he, the doctor, has a serious illness*', and when that doctor died: '*My God! Now I can't kill him any more!*'

SP showed none of the agonising guilt that so paralysed the Rat Man. He seemed to have managed any feelings, including sadness or guilt in relation to the suicides of his sister and father, or for his former analyst, frail and ill, by expunging them and being aware only of feelings of satisfaction.

Instead, he perversely filled himself up with excitement and triumph: he got rid of anything *dirty* through his daily enemas, though this left him anxious, suspicious of being cheated and delusional about the hole in his nose – no longer a mental one but instead a physical hole.

Noticing a mental hole would mean noticing who and what had been emptied from his mind: his fears of his rage and damage to anyone he might once have loved and needed, like the animals he mistreated, his depressed father, his sister, and his sick former analyst. It would mean becoming painfully aware of his emotional deprivation in the middle of such material wealth – in part contributed to by him.

Appendix F

Richard, aged 10 years (April to August 1941) (Klein, 1945,1961)

During the early part of the Second World War, Klein was evacuated to Pitlochry, in Scotland, where she saw Richard, an inhibited, phobic, 10-year-old boy daily for four months – and had time to take detailed sessional notes.

> Richard was inhibited, fearful of other children and unable to attend school. He clung to his mother in a childish way – seeing himself as her chick.
> As a baby he had feeding difficulties and his mother had found him an unrewarding baby compared to her elder son. Richard's mother was described as depressive and she did not seem to appreciate her son's musicality or his kindness. Richard's father was very deaf and a benign, but rather remote, figure. The family's London house had recently been bombed; in addition Richard had had a circumcision without warning.

Klein's records give a clear sense of the to and fro of analytic sessions: of anxieties interpreted, relief following and new, or renewed anxieties – again interpreted. She took up both Richard's loving feelings and his hostile ones towards her, his analyst in the room, as well as towards his parents. Klein spoke in a more literal, bodily way than is generally used now (Spillius, 1994) – but which Richard seems to have taken in his stride.

Klein had seen Richard for several weeks in daily sessions before returning to London for two weeks. In the first session back:

> Richard was anxious and listless: he barely looked at his analyst. He described the village they were living in as a 'pigsty'; was anxious about toadstools he found in the garden which might be 'poisonous'; and was dismayed to find in a book a picture of an 'awful monster'
>
> (Klein, 1961, p. 191).

Klein replied that she had now become a bad *pigsty Mrs K*, by her leaving him. This was made worse by his thought that she would be meeting up with her husband, like a Hitler/Daddy – which made him want to bomb her.

> Richard then showed a flood of relief and love for his analyst, her beauty, her silver hair, the mountainside . . .

In the next session

> *the boy bumped two of his toy ships together; Rodney, which represented his mother, and Vampire – which he said was himself.*
> Klein spoke of his wishes to have intercourse with his mother.

Richard then placed all the ships in an ordered row: his father, mother, elder brother, self, family dog . . . .

Klein said that he now wanted to keep the peace and give up his wishes for his mother.

He spoke of being his mummy's chick ... Chicks do run after their Mums ... but then chicks have to do without them, because the hens don't look after them any more and don't care for them.

Klein said that she had been away like the hen leaving her chick, and had changed in Richard's mind into a bad frustrating figure. He hated the frustrating her and his mother – and then worried that he had injured them.

Richard seemed momentarily relieved: he smiled; he now thought the 'awful monster' in the previous day's picture, would be 'delicious to eat'. But he then became listless and tired once again.

Klein told him she thought this was because he did not want to hear about such frightening thoughts.

Richard then drew an octopus, which had a long red section (Richard's colour) which, he said, was 'running through his mother's empire'. He then quickly changed his mind: it wasn't his mother's empire, but 'one which belonged to everyone . . .'

Klein said Richard was worried about having pierced his mother's empire.

He thought the red section 'looked like a genital'.

Klein said that on one side of the drawing there was the good, peaceful mother – but on the other side was the bad (and sexual) mother, linked with his dangerous father. He wanted to separate the two sides to protect his mother – but also out of jealousy.

In the next session:

Richard was anxious again, this time about a boy he felt threatened by in the hotel. He sucked on a pencil.

Klein said the pencil was like his father's good penis, which he wanted to suck on but also to bite, and his father then felt bad and dangerous, like the boy in the hotel who he had felt threatened by.

Richard then made a lively drawing showing a fish covering with a fin a baby fish – but for the first time he wasn't one of the babies. His father was represented as a small octopus among the rushes. There was a submarine, Sunfish, underneath the ship, Rodney (his mother). In the air there was a plane circling. He did not know where he was in the drawing.

Klein thought Richard was the son/Sunfish

– and he rather cheerfully pointed out how the periscope went into Rodney.

Klein thought that Richard had kindly given his father a place with his mother – but as a little baby/octopus. But in addition, his father was represented in the warplane, keeping on eye on what Richard was up to with his mother, just as Richard, too, kept a careful eye on his sexual parents.

> *Richard looked out the window: he spoke with pleasure of wanting to climb the mountain – but then he thought of the thunderstorm (which he feared) might break over the mountain; and his worry for the mountain.*

Richard wanted to find a way to not only be a 'baby chick' in relation to his mother; he wanted to find a way to feel that he had something good and exciting to offer her, that she would be excited by, too (as she somehow had not been excited by his musicality, or by his kindness). Richard wanted to be able to feel he could push up against her, challenge her, attack her without having to fear that he had destroyed her. He needed his father's help to do this: his pencil/penis – and his involved support.

Klein interpreted Richard's jealous, active desires for his mother, his fears of damage to her, and also his wish to protect, care for and give babies to her. She also described his loving and aggressive feelings towards his excluded father. By naming Richard's wishes: his genital, aggressive and sexual ones towards his mother and his wishes to get his father out of the way, Klein was saying *this is so. This is normal. Even if it is also conflictual and painful.*

Only when Richard could begin to accept that he had aggressive feelings as well as loving ones towards his (previously idealized) mother, his father, brother and his analyst, could he begin to feel that there was something more solid in him and in relation to his parents. And his parents felt more solid, too.

There were constant shifts from feelings of inhibition, to relief, to excitement and triumph, to one's of further anxious dread – but Richard's play freed up. The sessions ended sooner than was ideal, Klein returning to London. But the work helped Richard master his anxieties sufficiently to return to school.

Forty years later, Klein's biographer met the adult 'Richard'. Richard remembered that he always had quite a temper. But he described Klein as always sympathetic and when shown Klein's book on his treatment, and seeing the photo of her on the back cover, Richard kissed it saying *'dear old Melanie'* (Grosskurth, 1986).

References

Ainsworth, M.D.S., Bell, S.M. & Stayton, D.J. (1971). Attachment and Exploratory Behaviour of One-year-olds. In H.R. Schaffer (Ed.), *The Origins of Human Social Relations*. New York: Academic Press, pp. 17–57.

Athill, D. (2008). *Somewhere Towards the End*. London: Granta Books.

Auden, W.H. (1940). *Collected Auden*. London: Faber and Faber, 2004.

Barrows, K. (1999). Ghosts in the Swamp: Some Aspects of Splitting and their Relationship. *International Journal of Psychoanalysis*, 80: 549–561.

Barry, V. & Fisher, C. (2014). Research on the Relation of Psychoanalysis and Neuroscience. *Journal of the American Psychoanalytic Association*, 62: 1087–1096.

Bateman, A. (1995). The Treatment of Borderline Patients in a Day Hospital Setting. *Psychoanalytic Psychotherapy*, 9: 3–16.

Bell, D. (2018). *Turning the Tide: The Psychoanalytic Approach of the Fitzjohn's Unit to Patients with Complex Needs*. London: Routledge.

Bion, W.R. (1962). *Learning from Experience*. London: Tavistock.

Bion, W.R. (1985). *All My Sins Remembered; and The Other Side of Genius: Family Letters*, Francesca Bion (Ed.). Abingdon: Fleetwood Press. Reprinted London: Karnac, 1991.

Birksted-Breen, D. (1996). Phallus, Penis and Mental Space. *International Journal of Psychoanalysis*, 77: 649–657.

Blake, W. (1966)[1790]. The Marriage of Heaven and Hell. In G. Keynes (Ed.), *Blake: Complete Writings*. Oxford: Oxford University Press.

Brazelton, T.B. & Cramer, B. (1991). *The Earliest Relationship*. London: Karnac.

Breen, D. (1993). *The Gender Conundrum*. London: Routledge.

Bremner, J.D. (2005). Effects of Traumatic Stress on Brain Structure and Function. *Journal of Trauma Dissociation*, 6: 51–68.

Breuer, J. & Freud, S. (1893). On The Psychical Mechanism of Hysterical Phenomena: Preliminary Communication from *Studies on Hysteria*. *SE II*: 1–17. London: Hogarth.

Britton, R. (2005). Anna O. In R.J. Perelberg (Ed.), *Freud: A Modern Reader*. London: Whurr.

Brown, G.W., Andrews, B., Harris, T., Adler, Z. & Bridge, L. (1986). Social Support, Self-esteem and Depression. *Psychological Medicine*, 16: 813–831.

Burnside, J. (2007). *A Lie about My Father*. London: Jonathan Cape.

Carter, A. (1967). *The Magic Toyshop*. London: Virago.

Chasseguet-Smirgel, J. (1970). *Female Sexuality*. London: Maresfield Library; Karnac.

Cooke, R. (2006). Review: The Amis Papers. *Observer*, 1 October.

Crews, F. & Crews, F. (1995). *The Memory Wars: Freud's Legacy in Dispute*. New York Review of Books.

Dante, A. (2013). *The Divine Comedy*, Clive James (Trans.). New York: Liveright.

Day Lewis, C. (2004). *Selected Poems*. C. Day Lewis and Jill Balcon (Eds). London: Enitharmon Press.

Deutsch, F. (1957). A Footnote to Freud's 'Fragment of an Analysis of a Case of Hysteria'. *Psychoanalytic Quarterly*, 26: 159–167.

Di Ceglie, D. (2009). Engaging Young People with Atypical Gender Identity Development in Therapeutic Work: A Developmental Approach. *Journal of Child Psychotherapy*, 35: 3–12.

Di Ceglie, D. (2014). Gender Dysphoria in Young People. In H. Huline-Dickens (Ed.), *Clinical Topics in Child and Adolescent Psychiatry*. London: Royal College of Psychiatry.

Di Ceglie, D. & Freedman, D. (Eds) (1998). *A Stranger in my Own Body: Atypical Gender Identity Development and Mental Health*. London: Karnac.

Donne, J. (1896). Twicknam Garden. In *Poems of John Donne (Volume 1)*, E.K. Chambers (Ed.). London: Lawrence & Bullen, pp. 29–30.

Ede, H.S. (2008). *Kettle's Yard House Guide*. Kettle's Yard, University of Cambridge.

Edgcumbe, R. (2000). *Anna Freud: A View of Development, Disturbance and Therpeutic Techniques*. Hove: Routledge.

Ehrensaft, D. (2007). Raising Girlyboys: A Parent's Perspective. *Studies In Gender & Sexuality*, 8(3): 269–302.

Emanuel, R. (2002). On Becoming a Father. In J. Trowell & A. Etchegoyen (Eds), *The Importance of Fathers: A Psychoanalytic Re-evaluation* Hove: Routledge.

Etkin, A., Klemenhagen, K.C., Dudman, J.T., Rogan, M.T., Hen, R., Kandel, E.R. & Hirsch, J. (2004). Individual Differences in Trait Anxiety. *Neuron*, 44: 1043–1055.

Fanthorpe, U.A. (1992). A Hanging Matter: Neck-verse. *The Poetry Book Society Magazine*.

Field, J. (Marion Milner) (1986). *A Life of One's Own*. London: Virago.

Fonagy, P., Rost, F., Carlyle, J., McPherson, S., Thomas, R., Fearon, P., Goldberg, D. & Taylor, D. (2015). Pragmatic Randomized Controlled Trial of Long-term Psychoanalytic Psychotherapy for Treatment-Resistant Depression: The Tavistock Adult Depression Study (TADS). *World Psychiatry*, 14: 312–321.

Fraiberg, S., Adelson, E. & Shapiro, V. (1980). Ghosts in the Nursery: A Psychoanalytic Approach to the Problems of Impaired Infant–Mother Relationships. In S. Fraiberg (Ed.), *Clinical Studies in Infant Mental Health*. London: Tavistock.

Freud, A. (1967). About Losing and Being Lost. *Psychoanalytic Study of the Child*, 22: 9–19.

Freud, A. & Burlingham, D. (1974)[1944]. *Infants without Families and Reports on the Hampstead Nurseries 1939–1945*. London: Hogarth.

Freud, S. (1893). The Psychotherapy of Hysteria from *Studies on Hysteria. SE II*: 235–305. London: Hogarth.

Freud, S. (1900). *The Interpretation of Dreams. SE IV*. London: Hogarth.

Freud, S. (1905). *Fragment of an Analysis of a Case of Hysteria, SE VII*. London: Hogarth.

Freud, S. (1909a). *Notes Upon a Case of Obsessional Neurosis. SE X*. London: Hogarth.

Freud, S. (1909b). *Analysis of a Phobia in a Five-Year-Old Boy. SE X*. London: Hogarth.

Freud, S. (1913). The Claims of Psycho-Analysis to Scientific Interest. *SE XIII*: 163–190. London: Hogarth.

Freud, S. (1914a). Remembering, Repeating and Working-Through. *SE XII*. London: Hogarth.

Freud, S. (1914b). On Narcissism. *SE XIV*: 91. London: Hogarth.

Freud, S. (1915a). Observations on Transference-Love: Further Recommendations on the Technique of Psycho-Analysis III. *SE XII*. London: Hogarth.

Freud, S. (1915b). Thoughts for the Times on War and Death. *SE 14*. London: Hogarth.

Freud, S. (1917). Mourning and Melancholia. *SE XIV*: 235–258. London: Hogarth.

Freud, S. (1918). *From the History of an Infantile Neurosis. SE XVII*: 1–124. London: Hogarth.

Freud, S. (1923). *The Ego and the Id. SE XIX*: 1–66. London: Hogarth.

Freud, S. (1926). The Question of Lay Analysis. *SE XX*. London: Hogarth.

Freud, S. (1939). *Moses and Monotheism. SE XXIII*. London: Hogarth.

Freud, S. (1940). An Outline of Psycho-analysis. *International Journal of Psychoanalysis*, 21: 27–84.

Garland, C. (2002). *Understanding Trauma: A Psychonalytic Approach.* London: Tavistock.

Grosskurth, P. (1986). *Melanie Klein: Her World and Her Work.* London: Hodder & Stoughton.

H.D. (1970). *Tribute to Freud.* Manchester: Carcanet.

Holder, A. (2005). *Anna Freud, Melanie Klein, and the Psychoanalysis of Children and Adolescents.* London: Karnac.

Horney, K. (1935). The Problem of Female Masochism. *Psychoanalytic Review*, 22: 241–257.

Jaques, E. (1965). Death and the Mid-Life Crisis. *International Journal of Psychoanalysis*, 46: 502–514.

Jamison, K.R. (1995). *An Unquiet Mind.* New York: Knopf.

Kahneman, D. (1996). Eulogy for Amos Tvesky. @The Nobel Foundation.

Kahneman, D. (2003). A Perspective on Judgment and Choice: Mapping Bounded Rationality. *American Psychologist*, 58(9): 697–720.

Kandel, E.R. (1999). Biology and the Future of Psychoanalysis. *American Journal of Psychiatry*, 156: 505–524.

Kandel, E.R. (2006). *In Search of Memory: The Emergence of a New Science of Mind.* New York: Norton.

Kaplan-Solms, K. & Solms, M. (2000). *Clinical Studies in Neuro-Psychoanalysis.* London: Karnac.

Klein, M. (1940). Mourning and its Relation to Manic Depressive States. *International Journal of Psychoanalysis*, 21: 125–153.

Klein M. (1945). The Oedipus Complex in the Light of Early Anxieties. *International Journal of Psychoanalysis*, 26: 11–33.

Klein, M. (1961). *Narrative of a Child Analysis.* London: Hogarth Press and the Institute of Psycho-Analysis.

Klein, M. (1975). Envy and Gratitude. In *Envy and Gratitude and Other Works 1946–1963.* London: Hogarth.

Knight, F. (n.d.). *Be For Real.* Berkeley, CA: Peermusic III.

Lamm, N. (2014). *Second Graders React to Lammily and Other Fashion Dolls.* Available at: youtube.com/watch?v=Jue_JlxnPGM.

Laufer, E. (1988). The Female Oedipus Complex and the Relationship to the Body. *The Psychoanalytic Study of the Child*, 41: 259–276.

Layard, Lord R. (2006). *The Depression Report*. The Centre for Economic Performance, Mental Health Policy Group, London School of Economics.

Leichsenring, F. (2005). Are Psychodynamic and Psychoanalytic Therapies Effective? *International Journal of Psychoanalysis*, 86: 841–868.

Leichsenring, F. & Klein, S. (2014). Evidence for Psychodynamic Psychotherapy in Specific Mental Disorders: A Systematic Review. *Psychoanalytic Psychotherapy*, 28: 4–32.

Lemma, A. (2012). Research off the Couch: Re-visiting the Transsexual Conundrum. *Psychoanalytic Psychotherapy*, 26(4): 263–281.

Lopez, M.A. (2007). In *The Saturday Guardian*, 1/9/07. Available at: amis95.blogspot.com.

Lowe, N. (1994). *The Beast in Me*. Plangent Visions Music.

MacFarlane, A. (1975). Olfaction in the Development of Social Preferences in the Human Neonate. In R. Porter & M. O'Connor (Eds), *Ciba Foundation Symposium 33—Parent–infant interaction* (pp. 103–113). New York: Elsevier.

Mack Brunswick, R. (1928). A Supplement to Freud's 'History of an Infantile Neurosis'. *International Journal of Psychoanalysis*, 9: 439–476.

Masson, J. (1992). *Against Therapy*. New York: Flamingo.

McDougall, J. (1995). *The Many Faces of Eros*. London: Free Association Books.

Milner, M. (1986). *A Life of One's Own*. London: Virago.

Mitchell, A. (1996). A Puppy Called Puberty/A Dog called Elderly. *Blue Coffee: Poems, 1985–95*. Hexham, Northumberland: Bloodaxe Books.

Mitchell, J. (1974). *Psychoanalysis and Feminism*. London: Allen Lane.

Mitchell, S. (2003) *Can Love Last? The Fate of Romance over Time*. New York: W.W. Norton.

Murray, L. (1992). The Impact of Postnatal Depression on Infant Development. *Journal of Child Psychology & Psychiatry*, 33: 543–561.

Murray, L. (2009). The Development of Children of Postnatally Depressed Mothers: Evidence from the Cambridge Longitudinal Study. *Psychoanalytic Psychotherapy*, 23: 185–199.

Murray, L., Stanley, C., Hooper, R., King, F. & Fiori-Cowley, A. (1996). The Role of Infant Factors in Post-natal Depression and Mother–Infant Interactions. *Developmental Medicine & Child Neurology*, 38: 109–119.

Murray Parkes, C. (1986). *Bereavement: Studies of Grief in Adult Life*. London: Penguin.

Nabokov, V. (2012). *Lolita*. Penguin Modern Classics.

Natter, T. (2001). On the Limits of the Exhibitable. In M. Hollein & T. Natter (Eds), *The Naked Truth: Klimt, Schiele, Kokoschka and Other Scandals*. Munich: Prestel.

Pound, A., Puckering, C., Cox, T. & Mills, M. (1988). The Impact of Maternal Depression on Young Children. *British Journal of Psychotherapy*, 4(3): 240–252.

Pretorius, I.-M. (2010). Genetic and Environmental Contributors to the Intergenerational Transmission of Trauma and Disorganised Attachment Relationships. In T. Baradon (Ed.), *Relational Trauma in Infancy*. Hove: Routledge.

Proust, M. (1923). *The Captive. A la recherche du temps perdu, Volume V*. New York: Vintage Classics, 1996.

Raphael-Leff, J. & Perelberg, R. (2008). *Female Experience: Four Generations of British Women Psychoanalysts on Work with Women*. London: Anna Freud Centre.

Rilke, R.M. (1981). You See I Want a Lot. In *Selected Poems*, R. Bly (Trans.). New York: Harper Perennial.

Roth, P. (1969). *Portnoy's Complaint*. New York: Vintage.

Rothko, M. (2006). *Writings on Art*. New Haven, CT: Yale University Press.

Ryan, O. (2015). How Reading Can Change Prisoners' Lives. *Financial Times*, 17/04/15.

Schore, A. (2010). Relational Trauma and the Developing Right Brain: The Neurobiology of Broken Attachment Bonds. In T. Baradon (Ed.), *Relational Trauma in Infancy*. Hove, Routledge.

Schore, A. (2011). The Right Brain Implicit Self Lies at the Core of Psychoanalysis. *Psychoanalytic Dialogues*, 21(1): 75–100.

Segal, H. (1952). A psycho-analytic approach to aesthetics. *International Journal of Psychoanalysis*, 33: 196–209.

Segal, H. (1981). Psychoanalysis and Freedom of Thought. In *The Work of Hanna Segal*. Northvale, NJ: Jason Aronson, pp. 217–227.

Shakespeare, W. (2010). *The Winter's Tale*, J. Pitcher (Ed.). The Arden Shakespeare Third Series. London: A & C Black

Shedler, J. (2010a). The Efficacy of Psychoanalytic Psychotherapy. *American Psychologist*, 10: 98–109.

Shedler, J. (2010b). Getting to Know Me. *Scientific American*, November, 52–57.

Shevrin, H., Snodgrass, M., Brakel, L.A., Kushwaha, R., Kalaida, N.L. & Bazan, A. (2013). Subliminal Unconscious Conflict Alpha Power Inhibits Supraliminal Conscious Symptom Experience. *Frontiers in Human Neuroscience*, 7, doi.org/10.3389/fnhum.2013.00544.

Simm, K. (1989). *Four Hours in My Lai*. Yorkshire TV.

Spence, B. (1963). *Phoenix at Coventry. The Building of a Cathedral*. Glasgow: Collins.

Spillius, E. (1994). Developments in Kleinian Thought. *Psychoanalytic Inquiry*, 14: 324–364.

Steele, M., Steele, H. & Murphy, A. (2010). The Adult Attachment Interview and Relational Trauma. In T. Baradon (Ed.), *Relational Trauma in Infancy*. Hove: Routledge.

Stein, G. (1959). *Picasso*. Boston, MA: Beacon Press.

Steinbeck, E. & Wallsten, R. (Eds) (2001). *Steinbeck: A Life in Letters*. London: Penguin Modern Classics.

Stern, D.N. (1985). *The Interpersonal World of the Infant*. New York: Basic Books.

St Exupery, A. (2012)[1945]. *Le Petit Prince*. Paris: Editions Gallimard.

Strachey, J. (1934). The Nature of the Therapeutic Action of Psycho-Analysis. *International Journal of Psychoanalysis*, 15: 127–159.

Taylor, D., Carlyle, J.A., McPherson, S., Rost, F., Thomas, R. & Fonagy, P. (2012). Tavistock Adult Depression Study (TADS): A Randomised Controlled Trial of Psychoanalytic Psychotherapy for Treatment-resistant/Treatment-refractory Forms of Depression. *BMC Psychiatry*, June: 12–60.

Thomas, D. (2014). *The Collected Poems of Dylan Thomas*. Centenary Edition. London: Orion.

Tronick, E.H., Als, H., Adamson, L., Wise, S. & Brazelton, T.B. (1978). The Infant's Response to Entrapment between Contradictory Messages in Face-to-face Interaction. *Journal of American Academy of Child Psychiatry*, 17: 1–13.

Tustin, F. (1986). *Autistic Barriers in Neurotic Patients*. London: Karnac.

Vergo, P. (1975). *Art in Vienna*. London: Phaidon Press.

Wallerstein, J.S., Lewis, J. & Blakeslee, S. (2002). *The Unexpected Legacy of Divorce: A Twenty-five Year Landmark Study.* London: Focus Press.

Webster, R. (2005). *Why Freud was Wrong.* Southwold: Orwell Press.

Welldon, E. (1989). *Mother, Madonna, Whore.* London: Heinemann.

Wilde, O. (1891). The Soul of Man under Socialism. In *Complete Works of Oscar Wilde.* London: Collins, 2003.

Wilde, O. (1893). *Lady Windermere's Fan.* In *Complete Works of Oscar Wilde.* London: Collins, 2003.

Williams, P. (2012). *Scum.* London: Karnac.

Winnicott, D.W. (1945). Primitive Emotional Development. *International Journal of Psychoanalysis*, 26: 137–143.

Winnicott, D.W. (1952). Anxiety Associated with Insecurity. In *Through Paediatrics to Psycho-Analysis.* London: Hogarth Press and the Institute of Psycho-Analysis.

Winnicott, D.W. (1953). Transitional Objects and Transitional Phenomena—A study of the first not-me possession. *International Journal of Psychoanalysis*, 34: 89–97.

Winnicott, D.W. (1958). The Capacity to be Alone. *International Journal of Psycho-analysis*, 39: 416–420

Winnicott, D.W. (1960). The Theory of the Parent–Infant Relationship. *International Journal of Psychoanalysis*, 43: 585–595.

Winnicott, D.W. (1964). *The Child, the Family and the Outside World.* London: Pelican.

Winnicott, D.W. (1969). The Use of an Object. *International Journal of Psychoanalysis*, 50: 711–716.

Winnicott, D.W. (1971). Playing: A Theoretical Statement. In *Playing and Reality.* London: Tavistock, pp. 56–58.

Wise Brown, M. (1942). *The Runaway Bunny.* New York: Harper & Row (revised edn 1972).

Woolf, L. (1961). *Downhill all the Way.* London: Hogarth.

Yeats, W. B. (2000). *The Collected Poems of W. B.Yeats.* London: Wordsworth Poetry Library.

Young-Bruehl, E. (2008). *Anna Freud: A Biography.* New Haven, CT: Yale University Press.

Yovell, Y., Solms, M. & Fotopoulou, A. (2015). The Case for Neuropsychoanalysis. *International Journal of Psychoanalysis*, 96(6): 1515–1553.

Index

129; inevitable 125; managing 83;
    Oedipal 83
discomfort 31–2, 47, 110
dishonour 80
disillusionment 105, 107
disinterested analyst 18
disorganized 40
distant 2, 112; partner 86
disturbing thoughts 21
dolls girls 96
Donne, John 56–7
Dora 7, 24–6, 82
doubt 1, 26, 63–4, 125; self- 62, 104, 141
drawings into words 88
dreams 1, 7–8, 16–17, 65, 69, 76, 78,
    111, 132
dreamy 22
drinking 127
drug-taking 127
drugs 1, 36, 59, 90, 94

early adolescence: aggression and bullying
    in 97; changing body in 96–97; changing
    relation with parents in 94; and being
    cool 98; and body out of control 92–4;
    and cracking the egg over the parents
    head 94–5; and desirable bodies 92; and
    experimenting with a sexual partner 97;
    and feeling sexually desirable 95;
    and girl's first menstruation 93; and
    images of models and make-up 94; and
    independent relationship with a parent
    95; and losing physical touch with
    parents 92; and peer group relationship
    97; and puppy in the underpants 92; and
    seductive adolescent daughter 94–5; and
    sexual experimentation 94; and sexual
    feelings and fantasies 93; and social
    pressures 98; unformulated desires in 92
Ede, Jim 126–7
Edgcumbe, R. 39
education 98, 119
efforts 15, 17, 23, 61, 64, 89, 121;
    failed 125
Einstein, A. 2, 7
Eliot, T.S. 142
Emanuel, R. 115
emotion/emotionally: alive and true 18,
    142; available 59; conflict 7; control 135;
    cut off 39; deprived 11; digestion 47;
    disturbance 21; grounding 54; in touch
    24; intimacy 98; lacking 80; less

contained 47; less engaged 138; life
    8–9, 19; openness 70; pain 8, 130; and
    physically trapped 103; protecting
    against closeness 138; *pulverized* 52;
    quality 3; rescue 39; resources 137;
    responsive 40, 54; self 1; strain 132, 136;
    strength 117; *stuck and shitty* 52; truth 2;
    unavailable 59, 101, 117; uncontained
    baby 62; unreliable 62
empathic support 32
empathy 26
emptying out links within the mind 51
emptying out of mind 48
encouragement 123
energy 2–3, 8, 73, 81
England 7
engulfing 84, 98
enthusiasm 80, 83, 85, 89, 134; holding
    on 125–6
environment 37, 41, 54, 57
envy: and dread of loss 113; and hate 133;
    and jealousy 34, 57, 89, 109, 114, 121,
    129; and Oedipal exclusion 111; and
    resentments 85; of others 86
erection 25, 96
Erikson, Erik 107
Etkin et al. 12
Europe 7, 27
Evan 59
'even the so–called chores I turn to joy' 126
excited imagined powers 78
excitement 25, 36, 50, 52, 64, 76–7, 81,
    92–4, 98, 100, 103, 142
exclusion 10, 54, 73, 78, 87, 105, 111,
    115, 117
exercise 1, 135
exhausted irritation 118
expectations 18, 21, 93, 96, 101–2, 116
experiences 14, 17, 31–2, 47, 63, 97, 134,
    140; difficult 58; of parenting 110;
    rich 59
experimenting with a sexual partner 97
exploring sexuality and emotional
    intimacy 98
external change 129
external pressures 23, 32, 84
external stress 1
extreme fitness 128

Facebook 97
facing our flaws 71
facing up to limitations 126

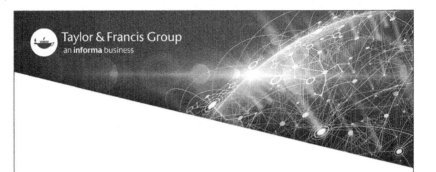

Made in the USA
Monee, IL
15 April 2021

65861527R00105